lobster is the best medicine

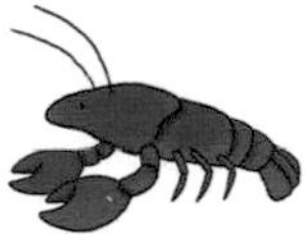

a collection of comics about friendship

by liz climo

RUNNING PRESS
PHILADELPHIA

for my friends
(and your friends, too)

© 2015 by Liz Climo
Published by Running Press Book Publishers
An Imprint of Perseus Books, LLC.
A Subsidiary of Hachette Book Group, Inc.

Printed in China
LEO

Books published by Running Press are available at special discounts for bulk purchases in the United States by corporations, institutions, and other organizations. For more information, please contact the Special Markets Department at the Perseus Books Group, 2300 Chestnut Street, Suite 200, Philadelphia, PA 19103, or call (800) 810-4145, ext. 5000, or e-mail special.markets@perseusbooks.com.

ISBN 978-0-7624-5868-4
Library of Congress Control Number: 2015936003

E-book ISBN 978-0-7624-5882-0

13   12   11   10
Digit on the right indicates the number of this printing

Designed by Ashley Haag
Edited by Jennifer Kasius
Typography: Avenir, Draftsman Casual

Running Press Book Publishers
2300 Chestnut Street
Philadelphia, PA 19103-4371

Visit us on the web!
www.runningpress.com

Introduction

When I was 23 I moved to Los Angeles and slept on my friend Andrea's futon for about three months. We both grew up in northern California, but she had moved to L.A. a couple of years prior. When I called and told her I had accepted a job on *The Simpsons*, and that I started in a couple of days but had no money saved and no place to live, she said without hesitation, "Great! Come stay with me! You can sleep on my futon." So that's exactly what I did. While this was a very exciting time for me, it was a lonely one too. I left some of my best friends behind when I moved, friends I worried I would lose touch with. I started my new job and listened as my coworkers talked in the hallway and made lunch plans. I missed my group of friends in northern California, I missed my family, and I was terrified to start my new life in L.A.. But at the end of the day, I had Andrea to keep me company and her futon to sleep on, so I knew everything would be okay. Ten years later, I am still in L.A., Andrea has moved to New York, I see my northern California friends every summer, I have an amazing group of friends here in Los Angeles, and a futon of my very own in case any of them ever needs a place to sleep.

I love my friends, and I started drawing these comics as a way to make them laugh. After wasting so much time worrying if my drawings were any good, I realized I actually don't care as long as they make my friends happy, because that's exactly how my friends make me feel every day. And now, hopefully, they'll make your friends happy too! So if you've picked up this book and haven't put it down yet (thanks, by the way!) consider giving it to an old friend, or a new friend, or just keep it for yourself. And if you're in a new place, starting a new journey, or even feeling a bit lonely, hopefully these comics will keep you company for a bit and make you smile.

Liz Climo

a friend in need

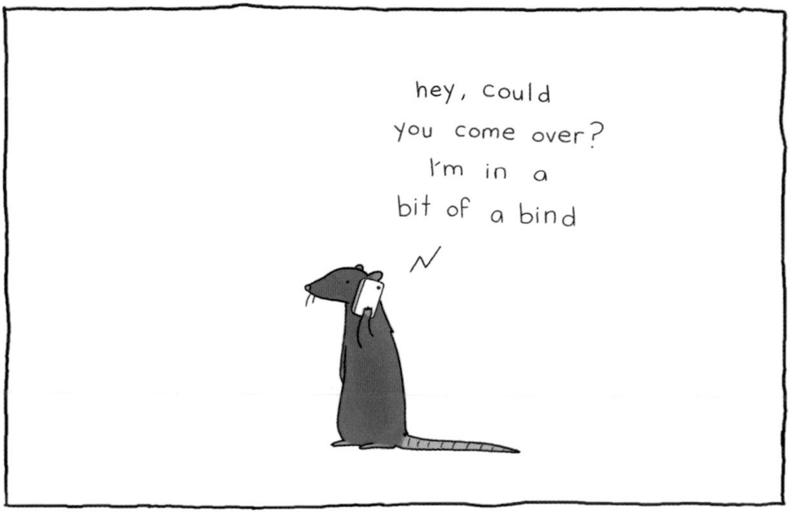
hey, could you come over? I'm in a bit of a bind

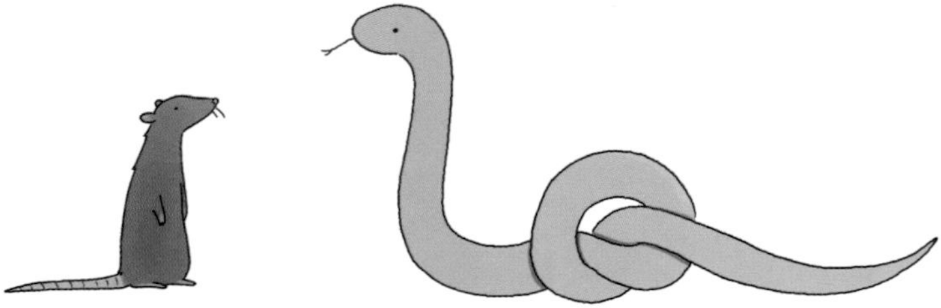

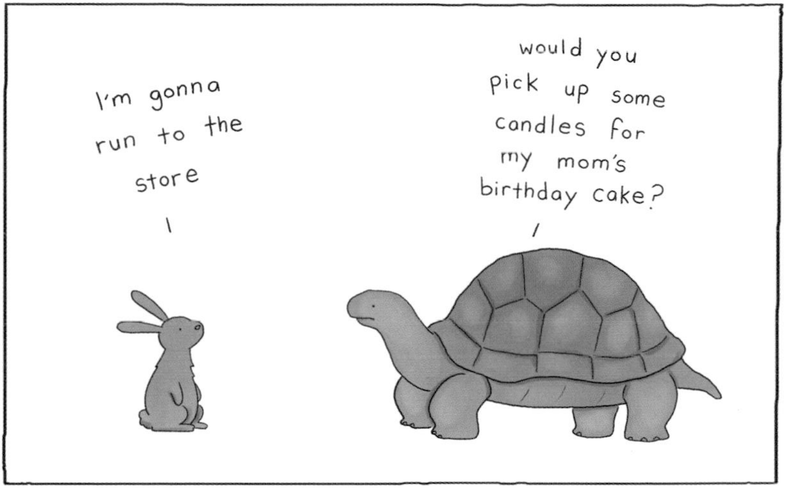
I'm gonna run to the store
would you pick up some candles for my mom's birthday cake?

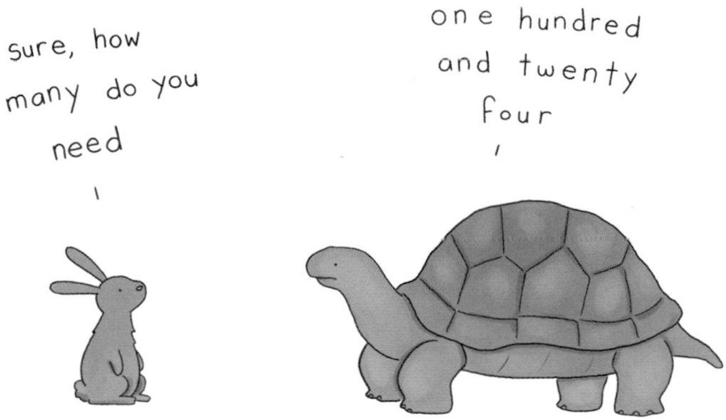
sure, how many do you need
one hundred and twenty four

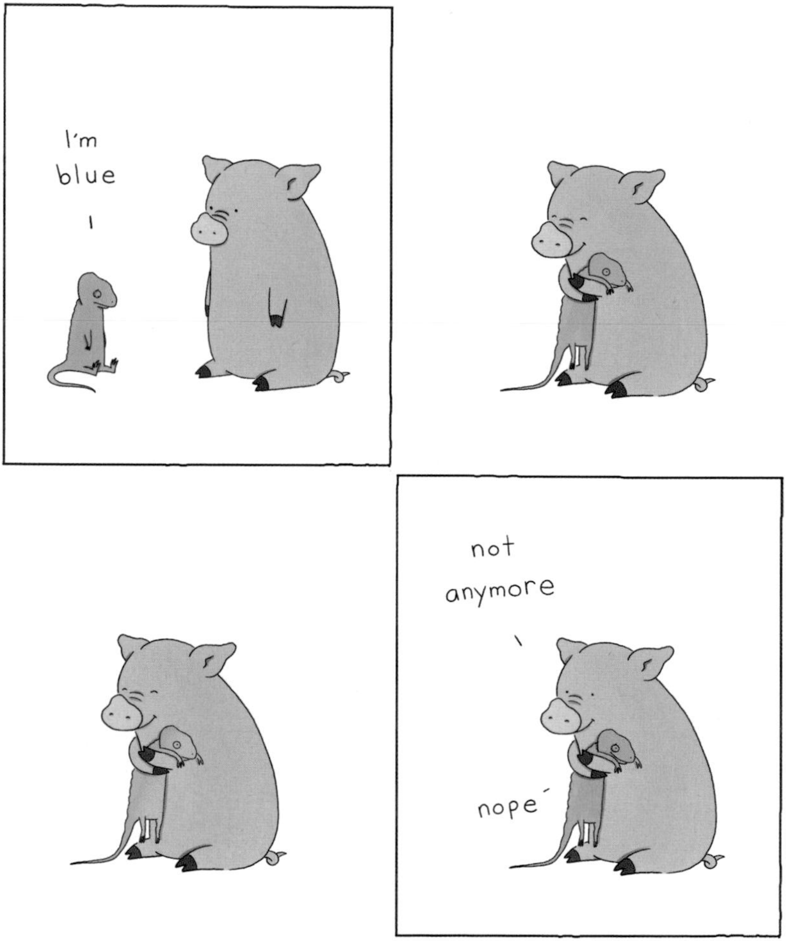
I'm blue
not anymore
nope

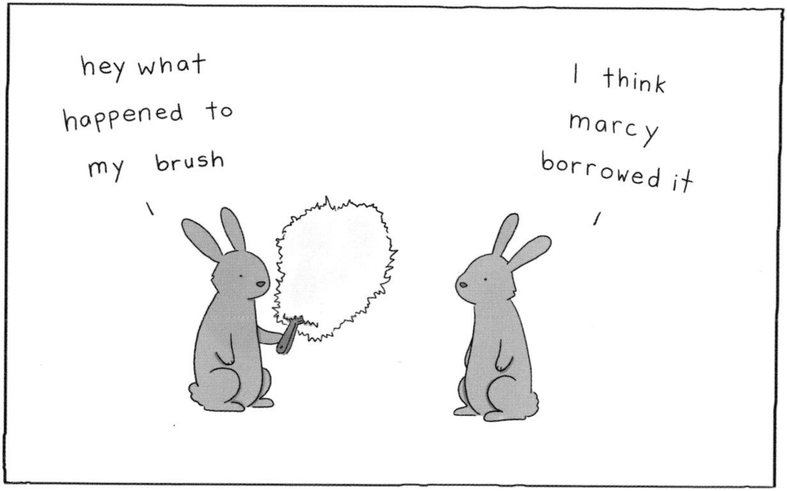
hey what happened to my brush
I think marcy borrowed it

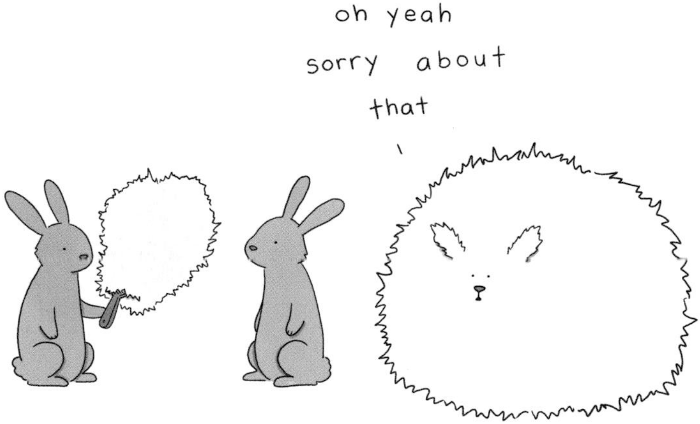
oh yeah sorry about that

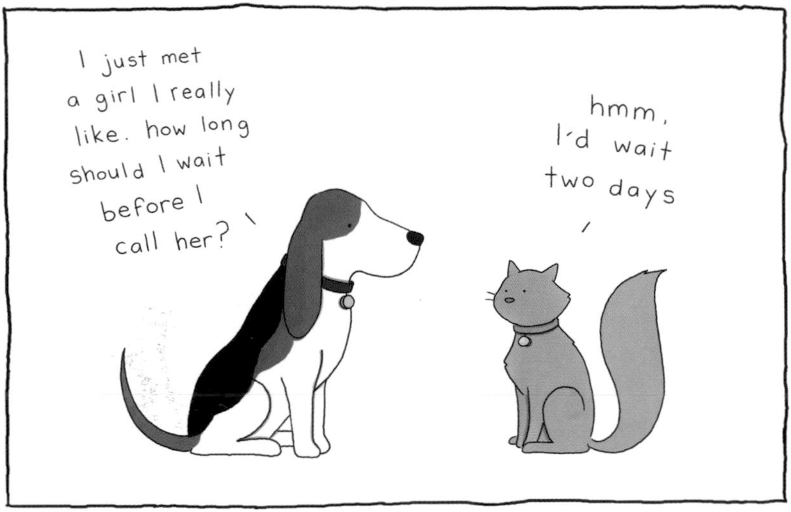
I just met a girl I really like. how long should I wait before I call her?
hmm, I'd wait two days

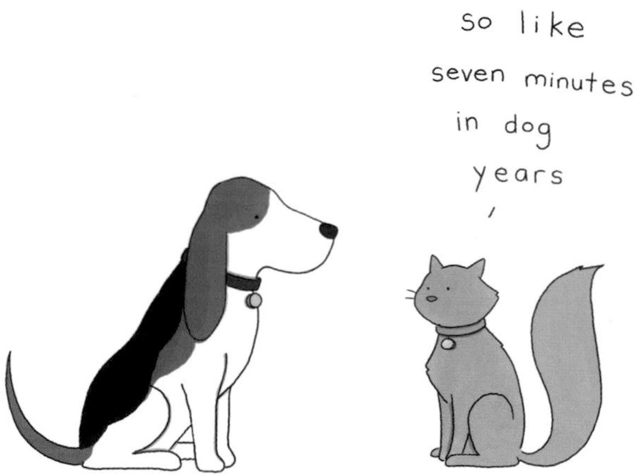
so like seven minutes in dog years

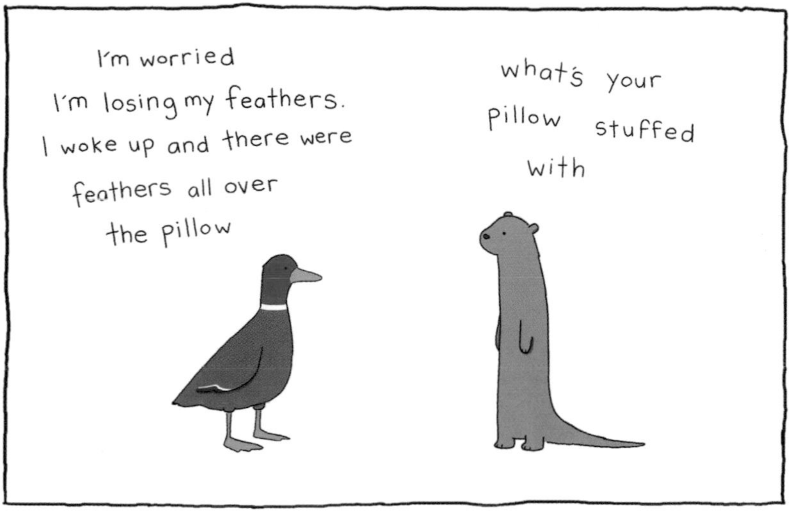
I'm worried I'm losing my feathers. I woke up and there were feathers all over the pillow
what's your pillow stuffed with

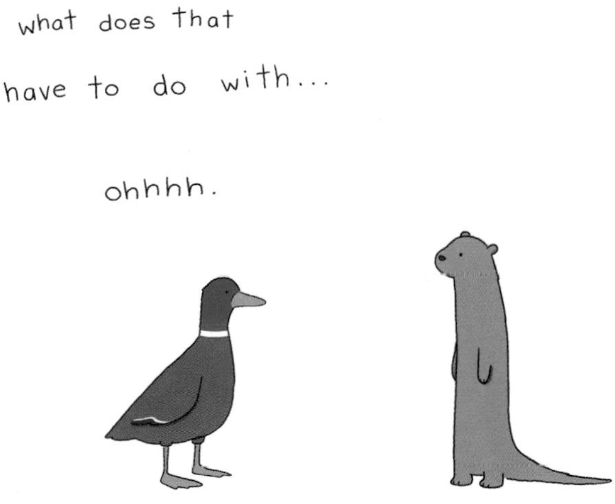
what does that have to do with...
ohhhh.

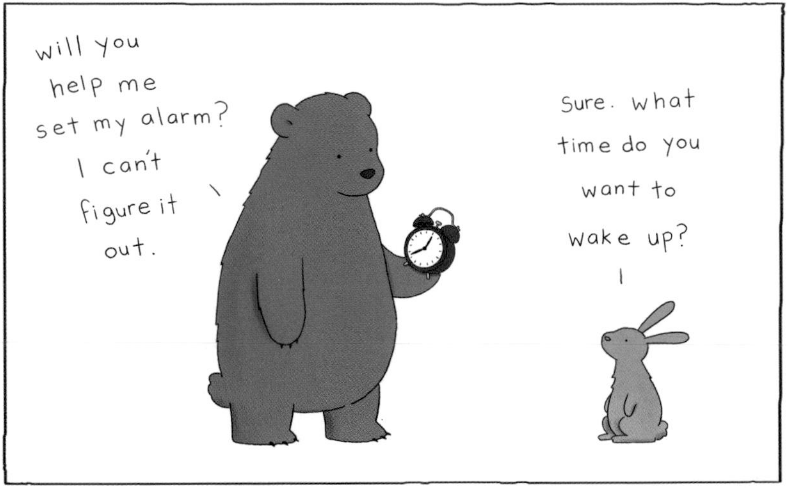
will you help me set my alarm? I can't figure it out.
Sure. what time do you want to wake up?

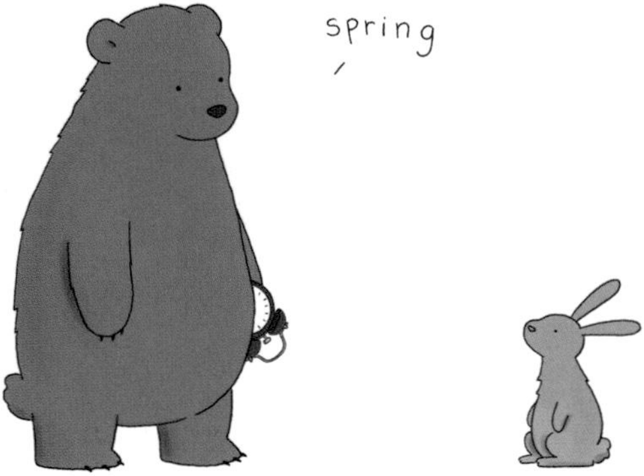
spring

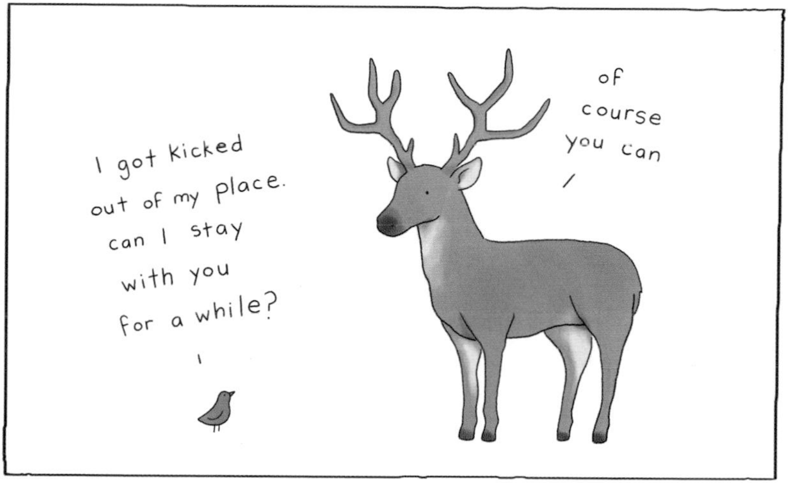
I got kicked out of my place. can I stay with you for a while?
of course you can

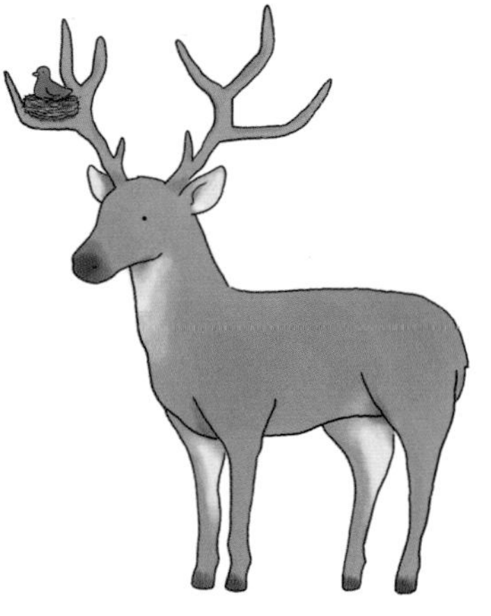

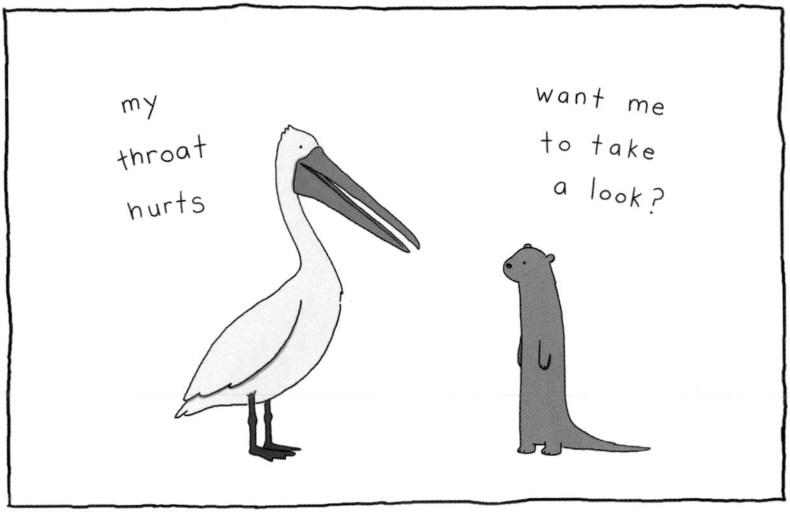
my throat hurts
want me to take a look?

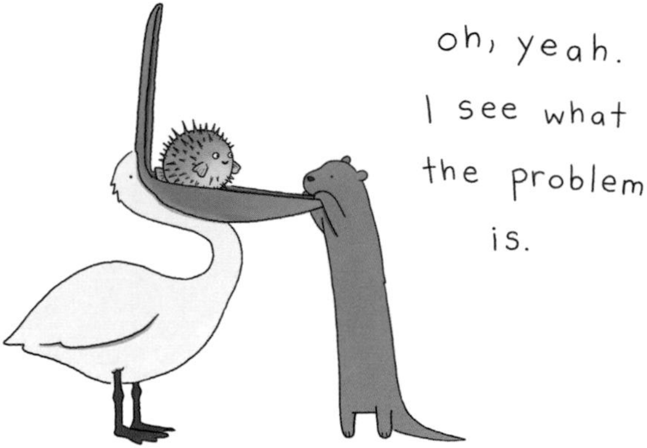
oh, yeah. I see what the problem is.

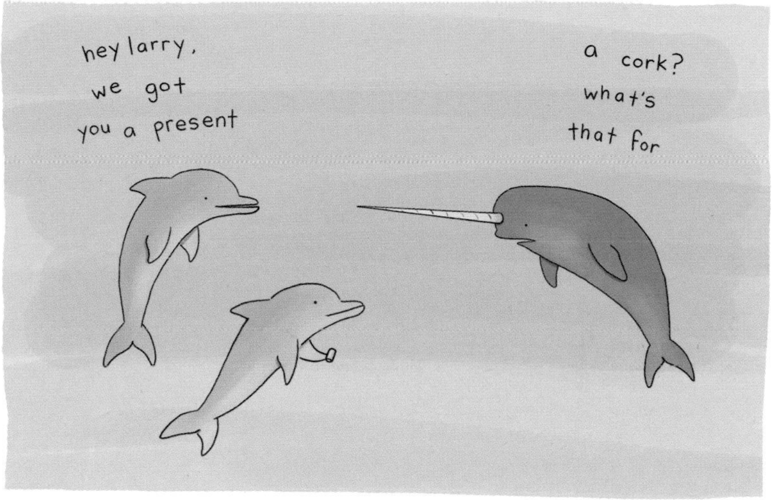
hey larry,
we got
you a present
a cork?
what's
that for

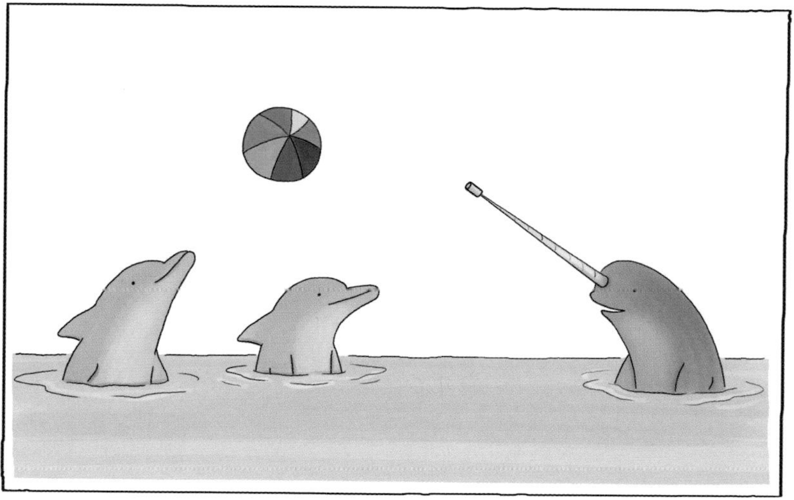

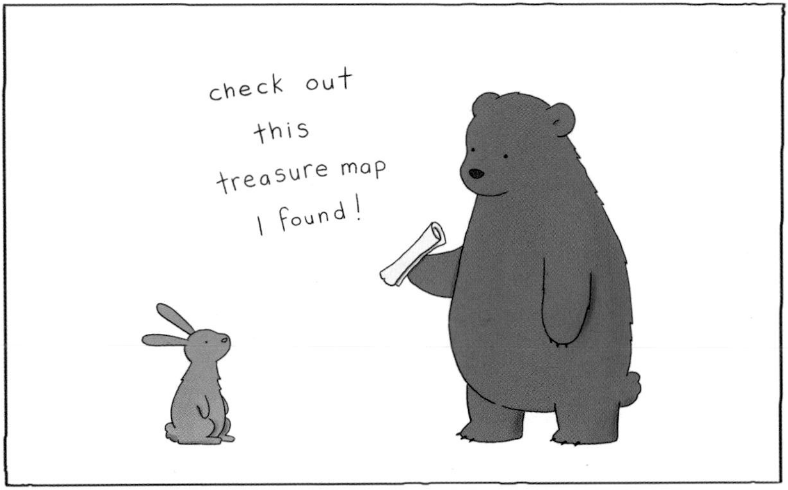
check out this treasure map I found!

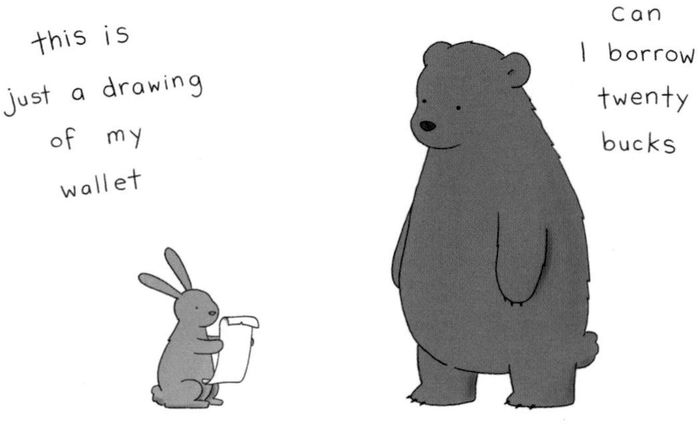
this is just a drawing of my wallet
can I borrow twenty bucks

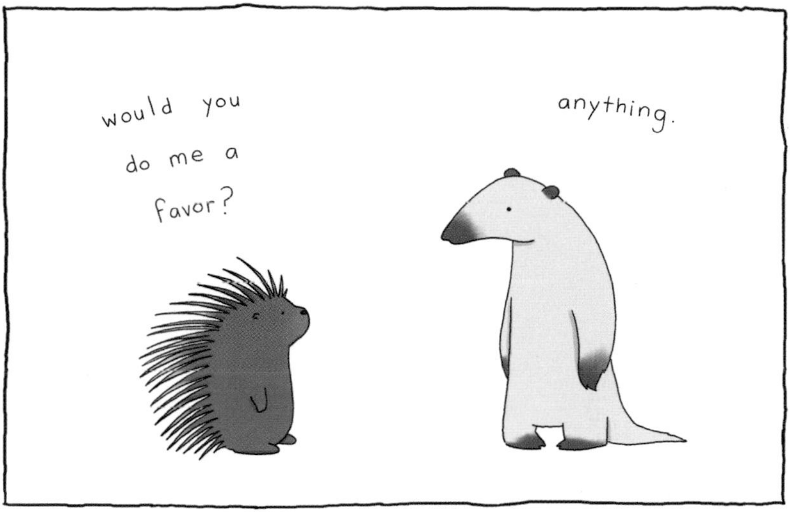
would you do me a favor?
anything.

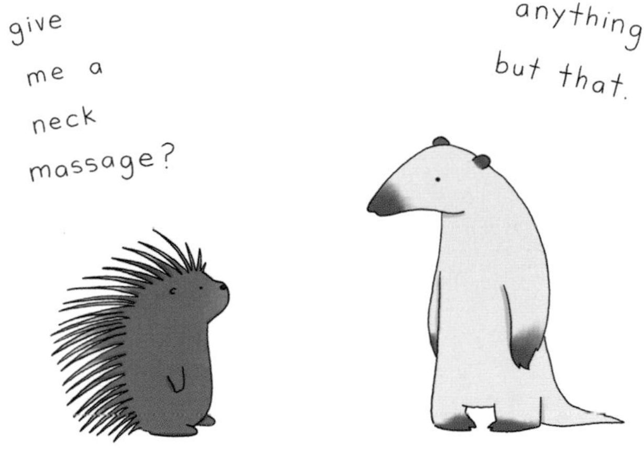
give me a neck massage?
anything but that.

don't worry.
there are
plenty of fish
in the sea.

dude,
dolphins
aren't fish.

do you need a shoulder to cry on?
you don't have shoulders.

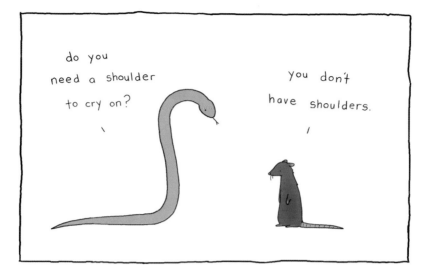

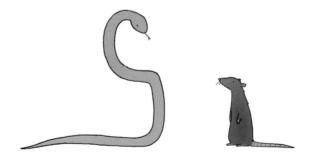

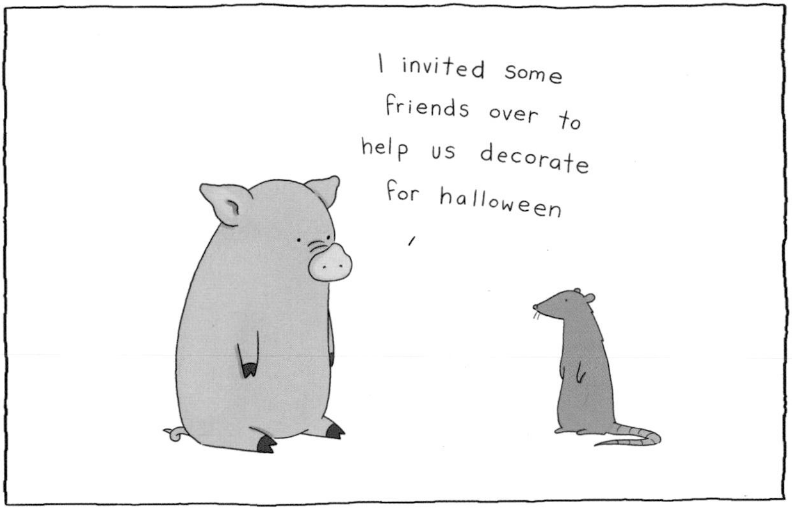
I invited some friends over to help us decorate for halloween

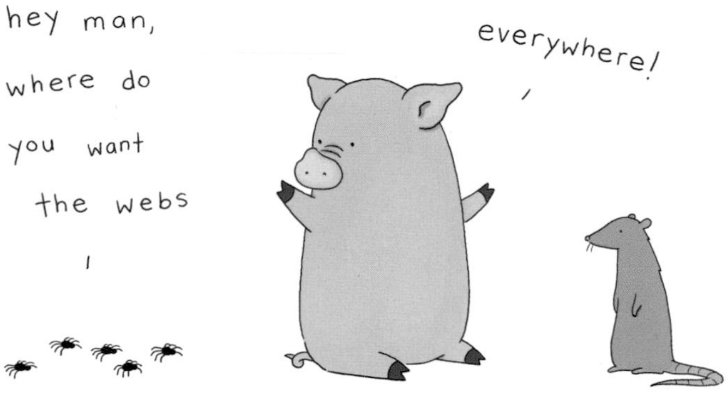
hey man, where do you want the webs
everywhere!

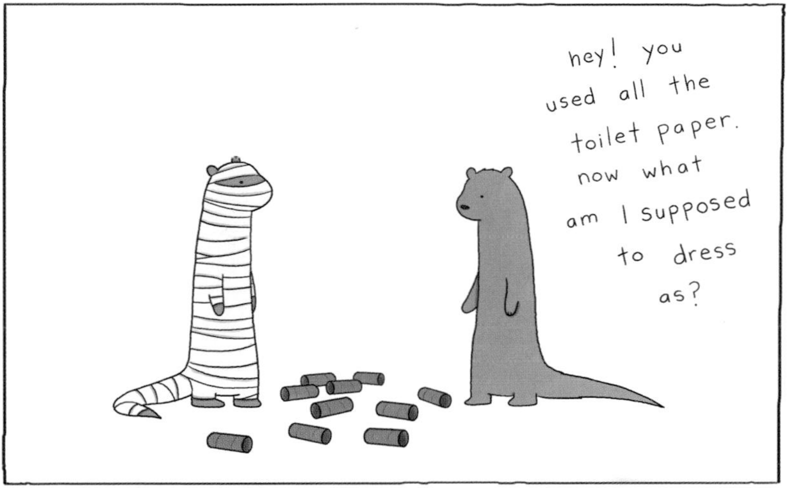
hey! you used all the toilet paper. now what am I supposed to dress as?

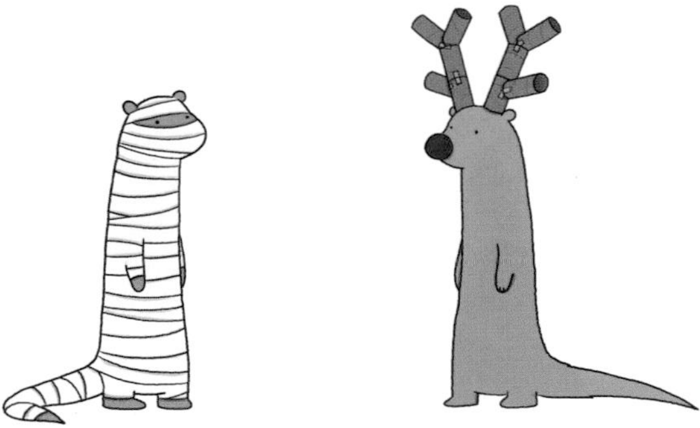

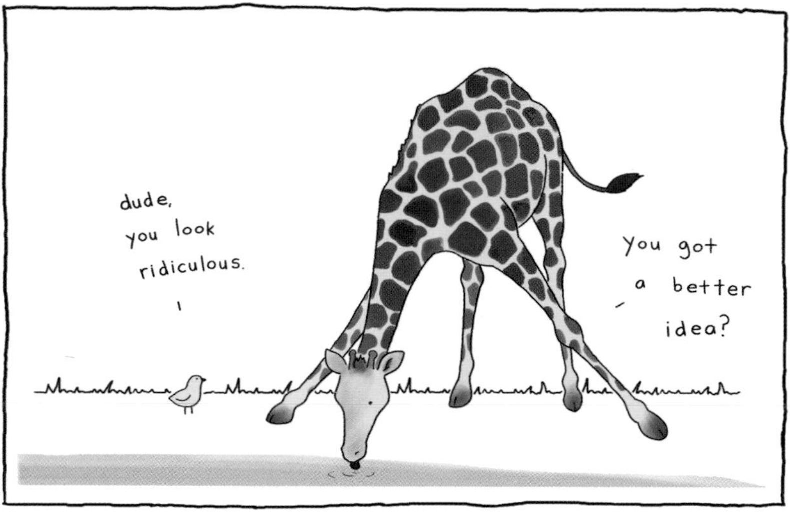
dude,
you look
ridiculous.
you got
a better
idea?

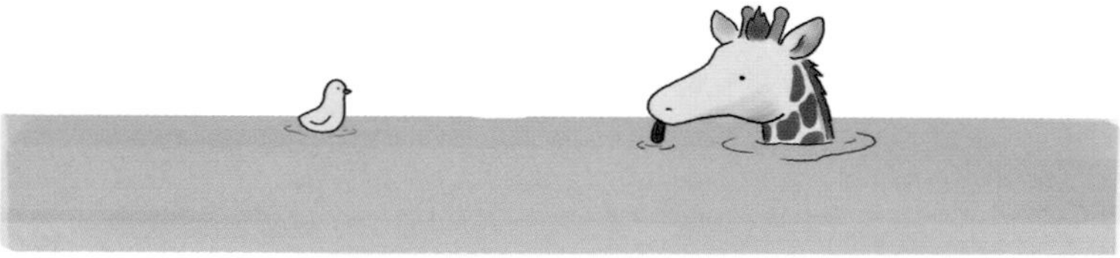

it's too hot.
my ice cream
is melting

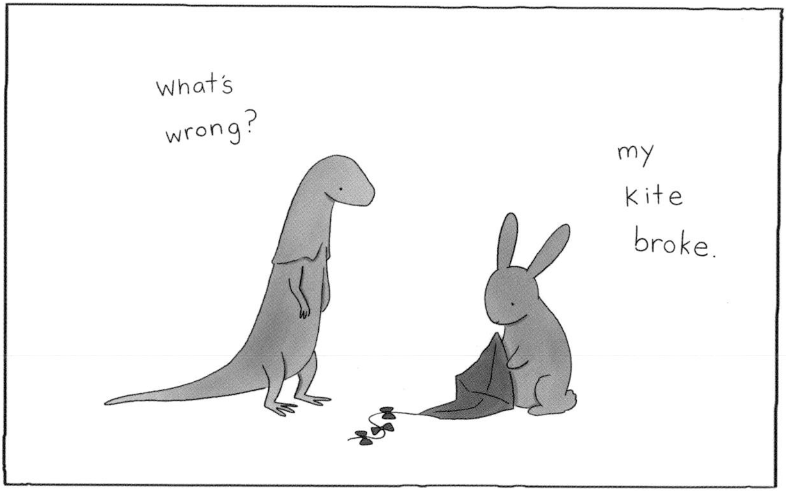
what's wrong?
my kite broke.

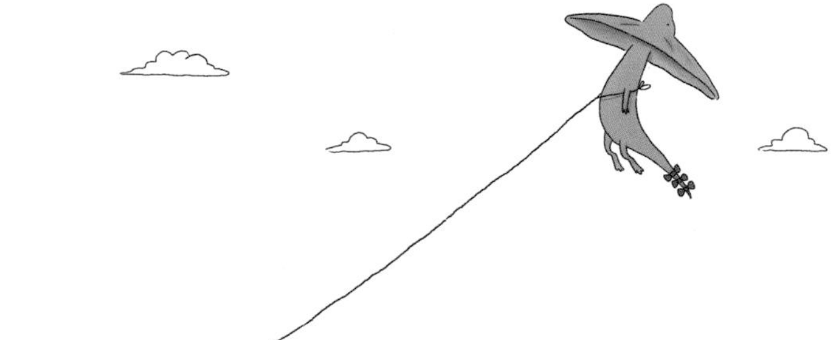

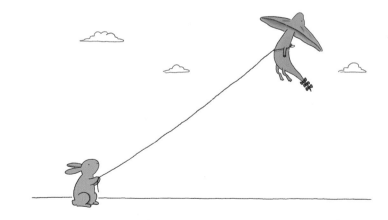

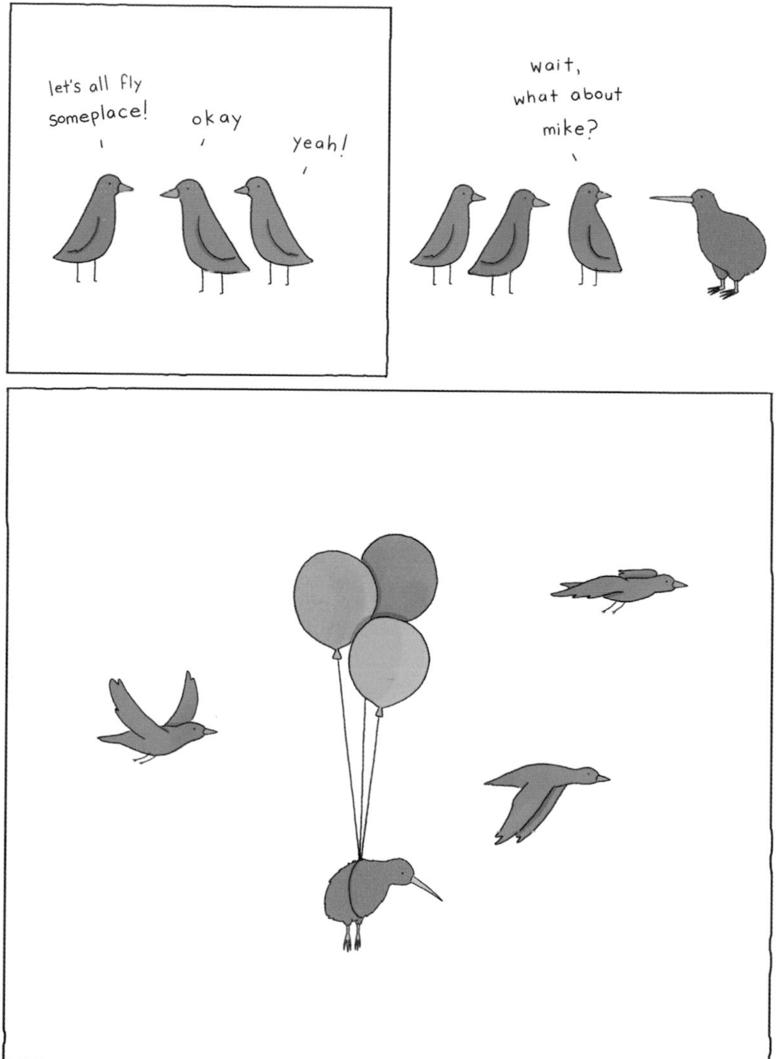
let's all fly someplace!
okay
yeah!
wait, what about mike?

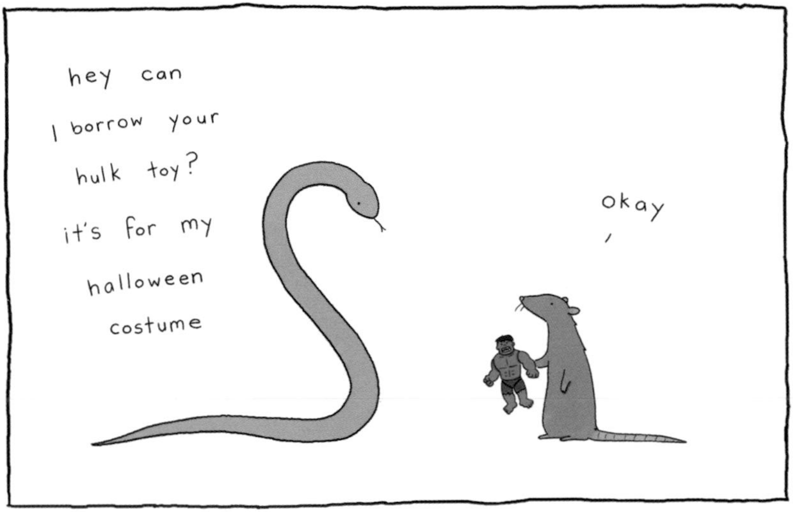
hey can
I borrow your
hulk toy?
it's for my
halloween
costume
okay

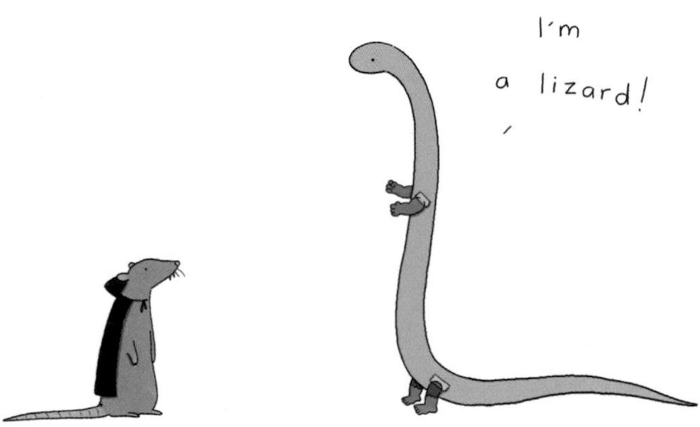
I'm
a lizard!

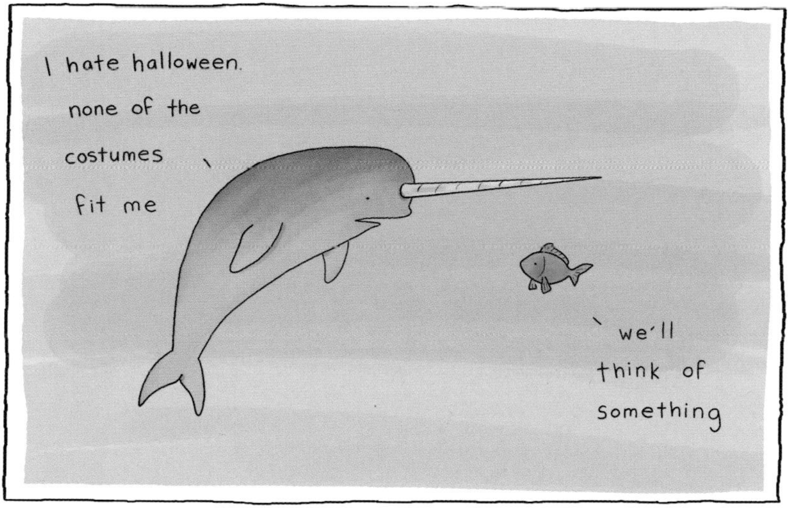
I hate halloween.
none of the costumes fit me
we'll think of something

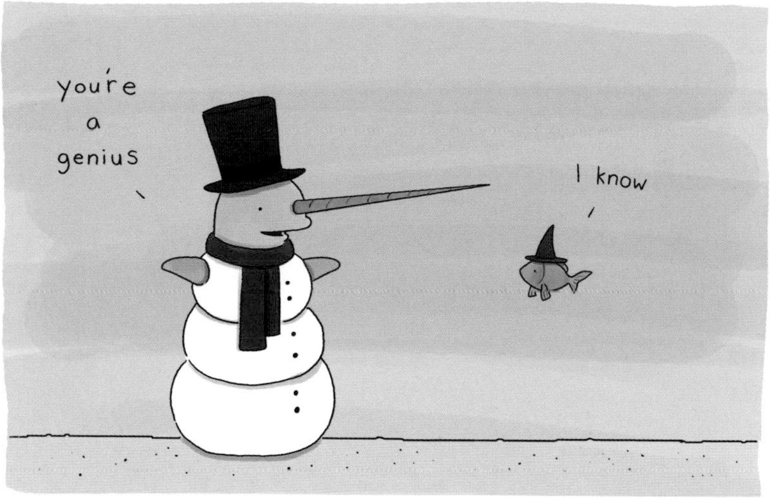
you're a genius
I know

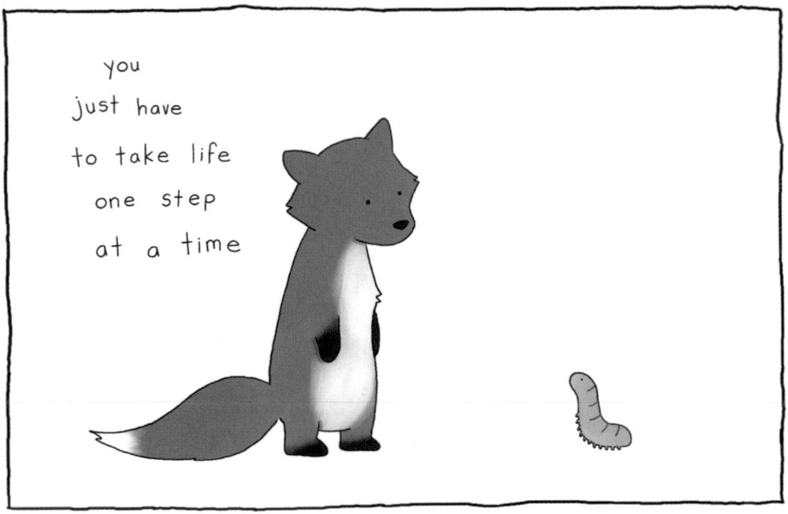
you
just have
to take life
one step
at a time

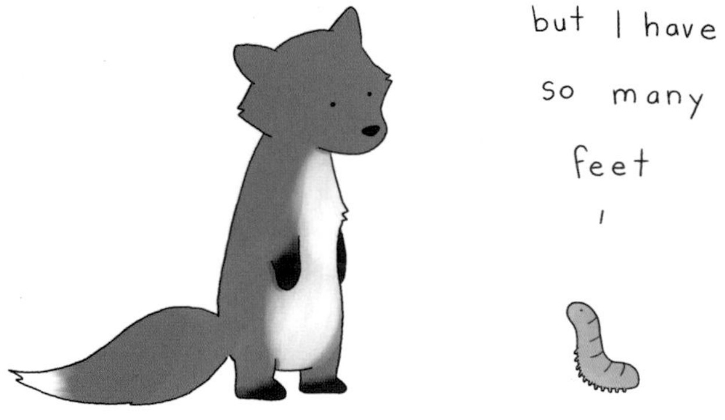
but I have
so many
feet

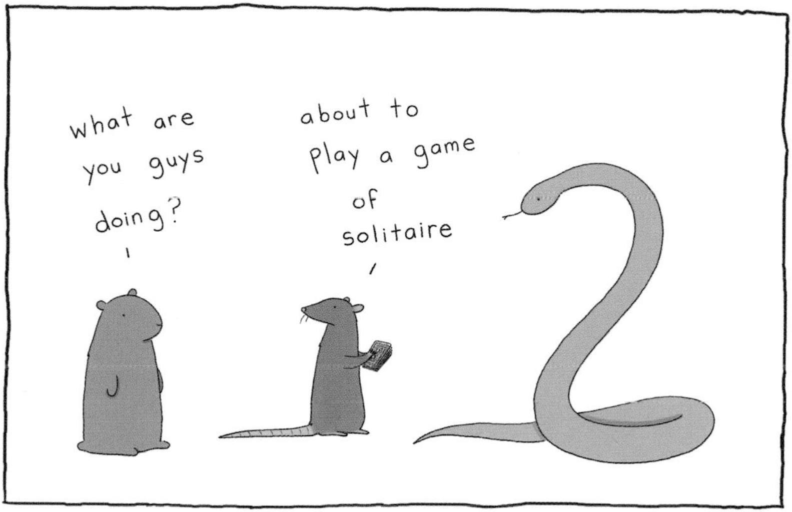
what are you guys doing?
about to play a game of solitaire

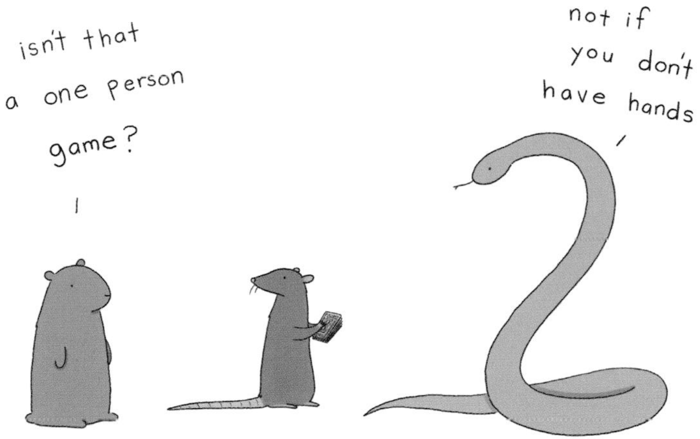
isn't that a one person game?
not if you don't have hands

I wanna
swing too.
but we don't
all fit.

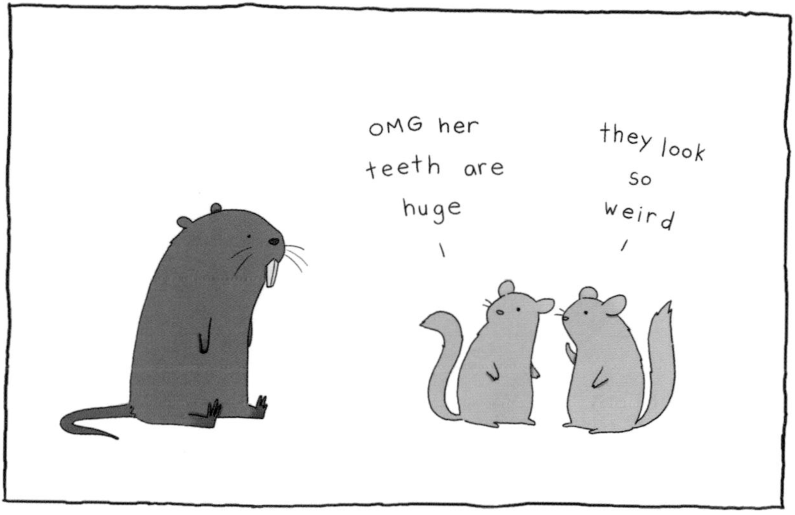
OMG her teeth are huge
they look so weird

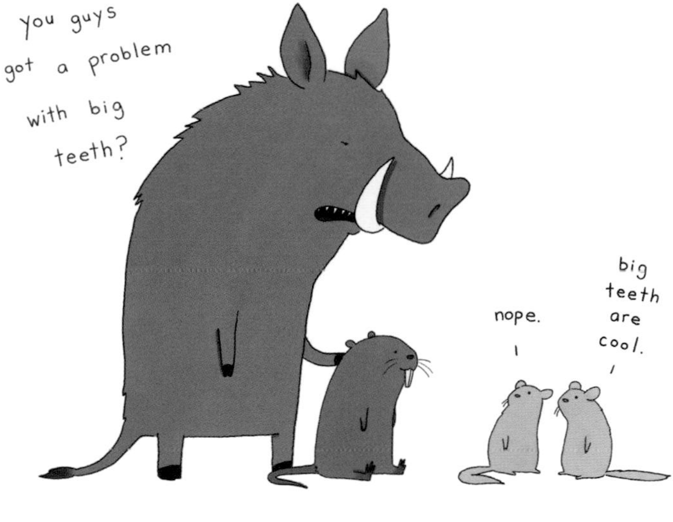
you guys got a problem with big teeth?
nope.
big teeth are cool.

best friends
forever

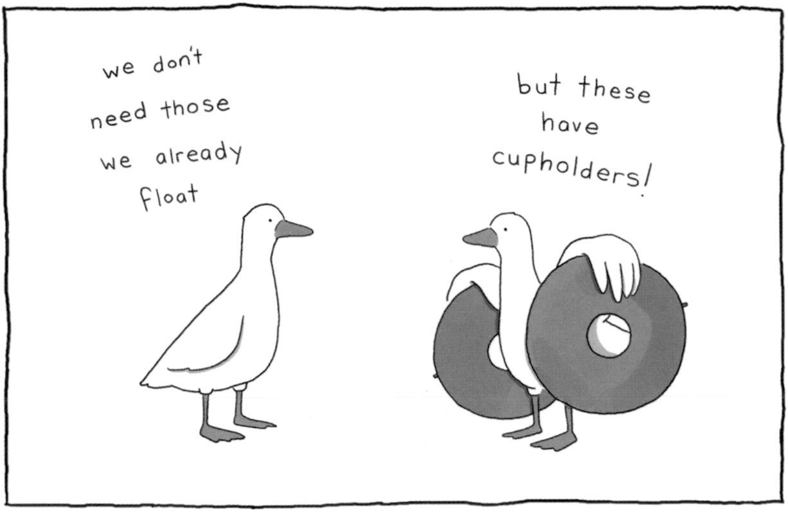
we don't need those we already float
but these have cupholders!

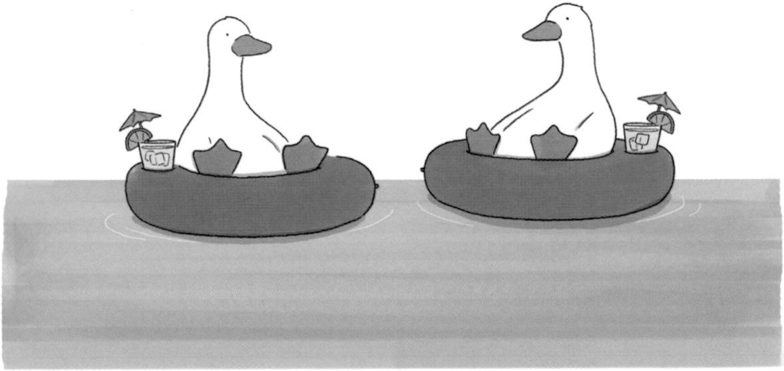

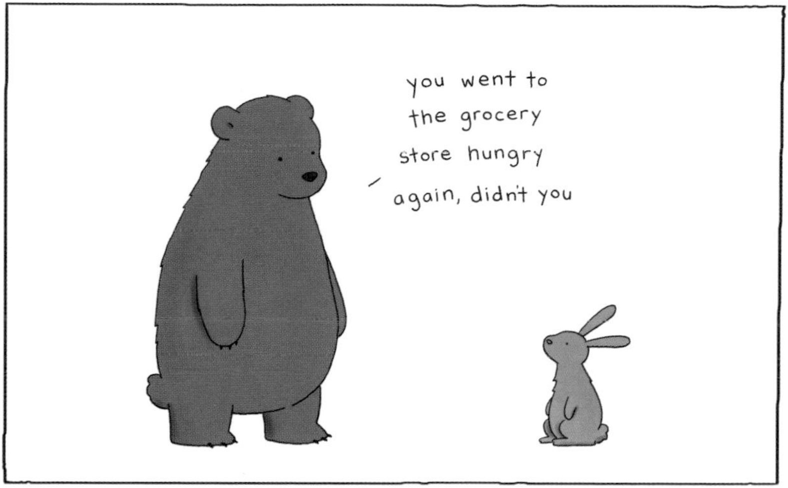
you went to the grocery store hungry again, didn't you

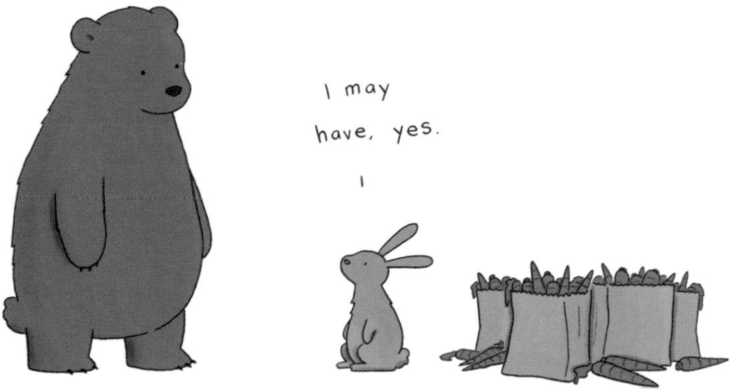
I may have, yes.

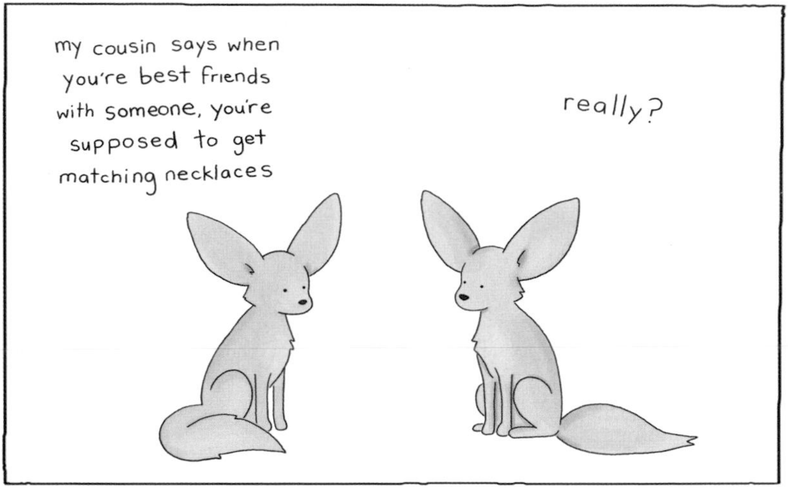
my cousin says when you're best friends with someone, you're supposed to get matching necklaces
really?

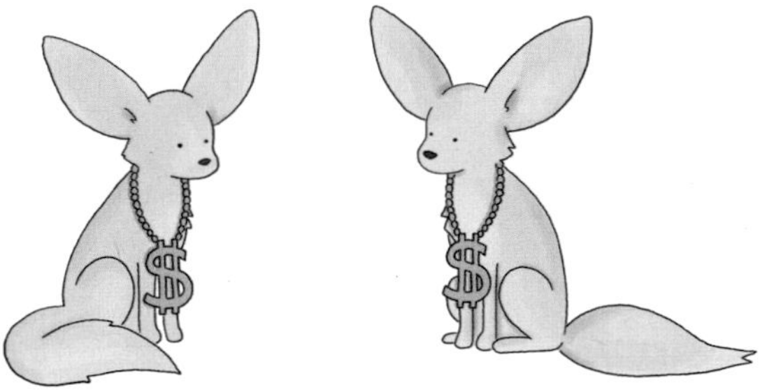

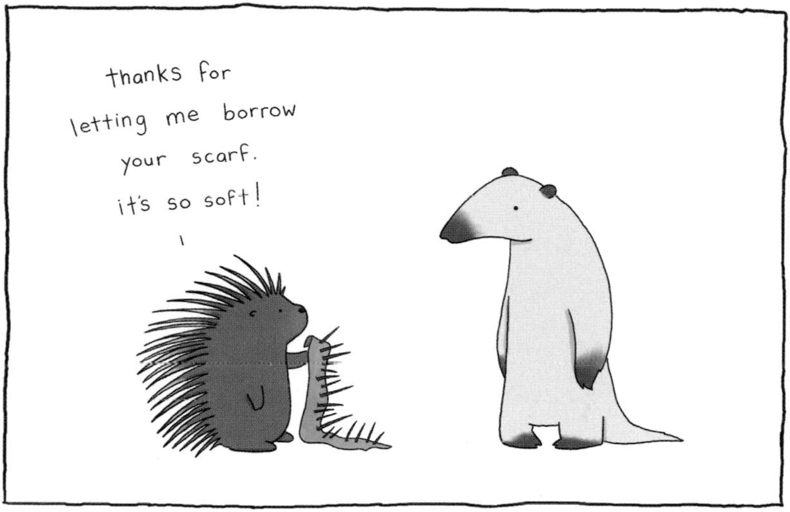
thanks for letting me borrow your scarf. it's so soft!

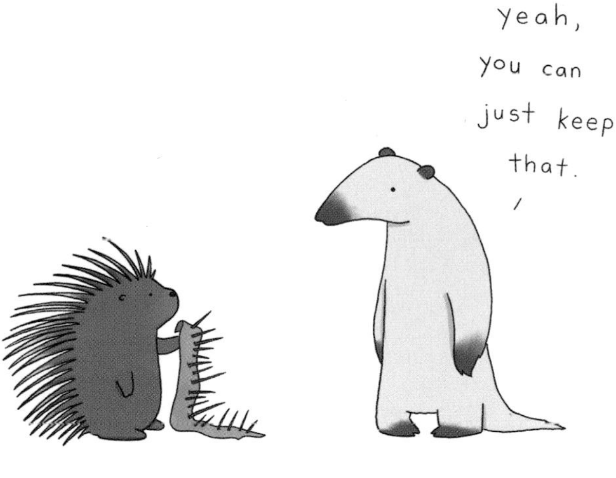
yeah, you can just keep that.

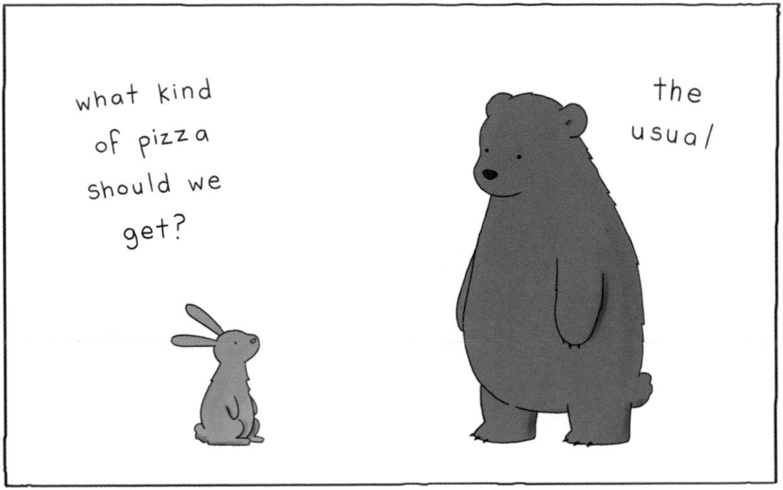
what kind of pizza should we get?
the usual

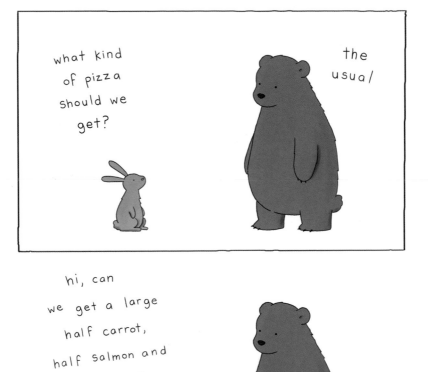

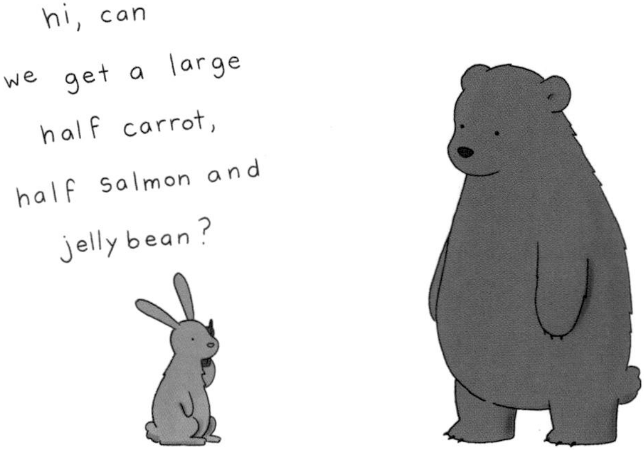
hi, can we get a large half carrot, half salmon and jellybean?

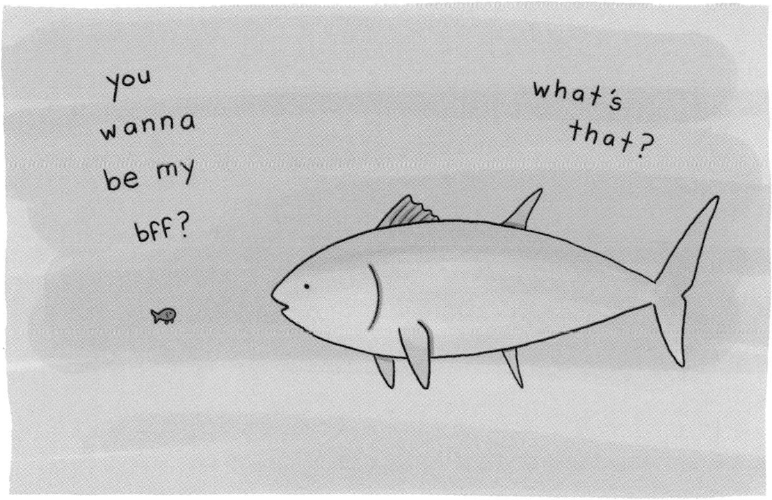
you wanna be my bff?
what's that?

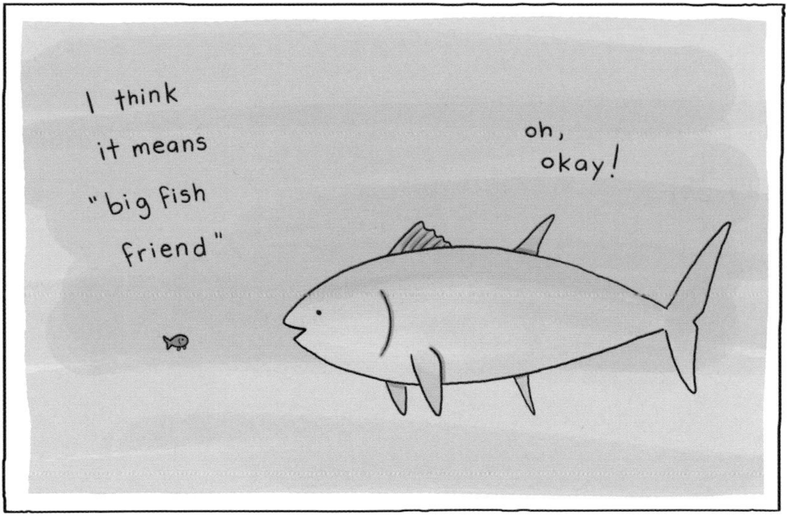
I think it means "big fish friend"
oh, okay!

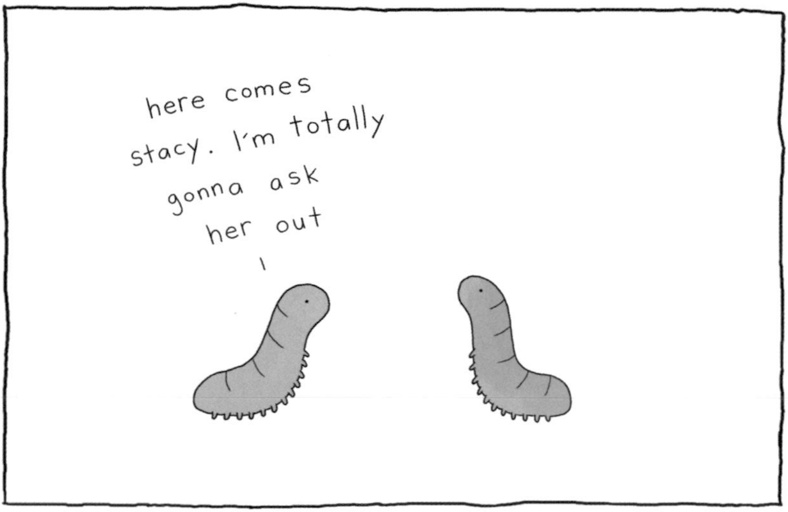
here comes stacy. I'm totally gonna ask her out

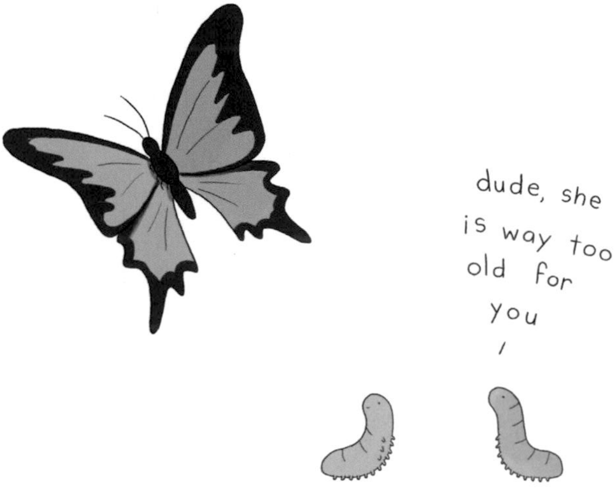
dude, she is way too old for you

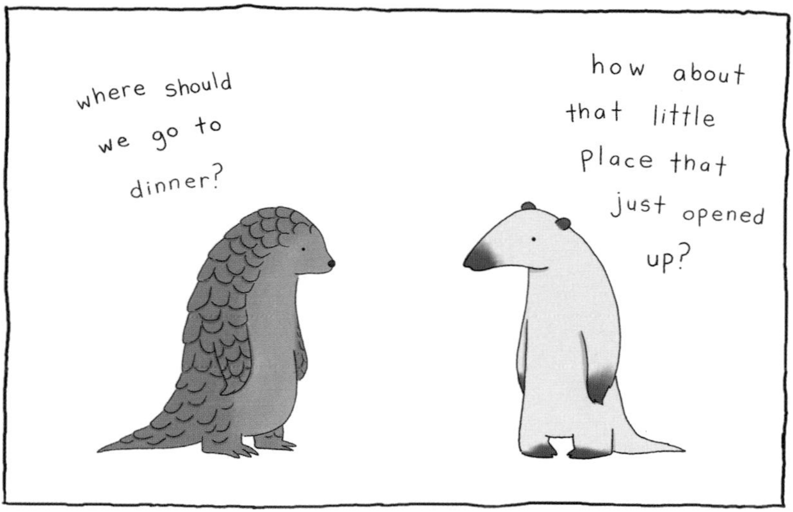
where should we go to dinner?
how about that little place that just opened up?

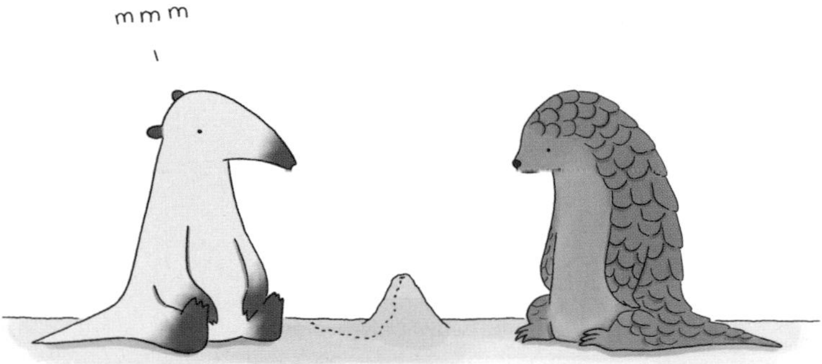
mmm

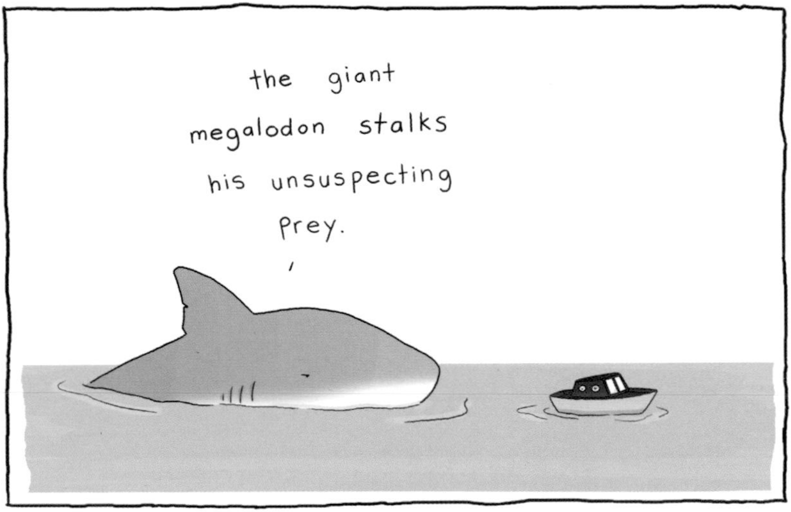
the giant megalodon stalks his unsuspecting prey.

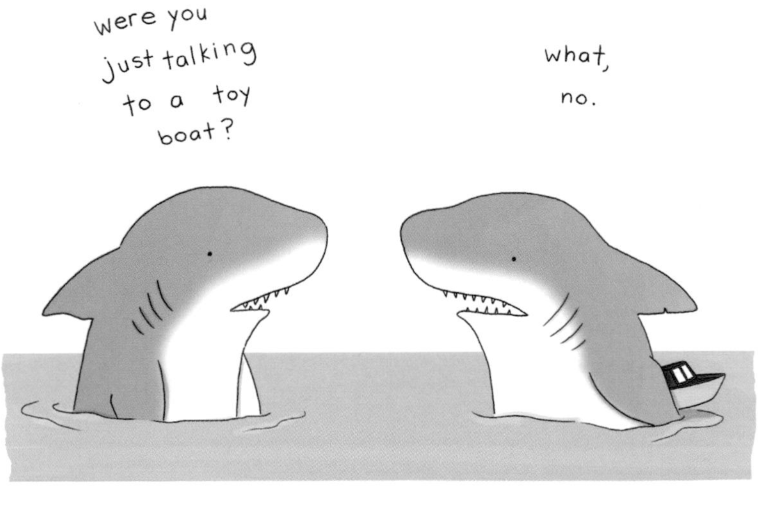
were you just talking to a toy boat?
what, no.

it's gonna
be cold
tonight

we should
wear
leg warmers

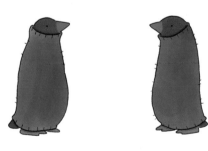

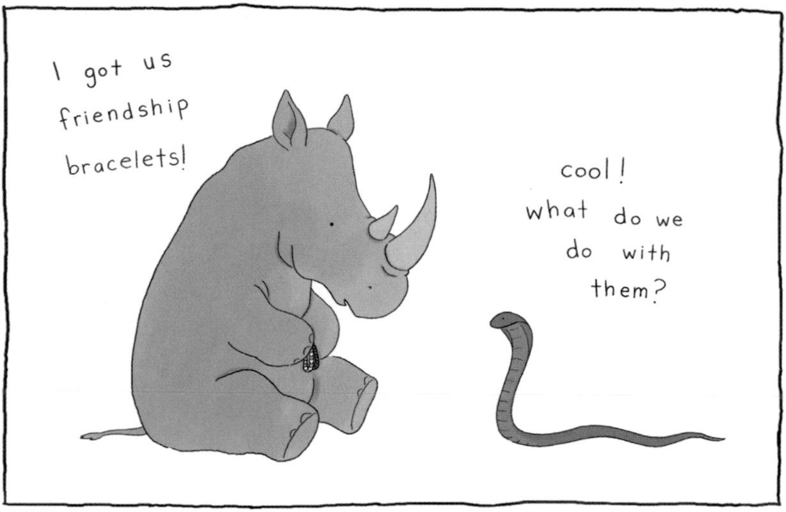
I got us friendship bracelets!
cool! what do we do with them?

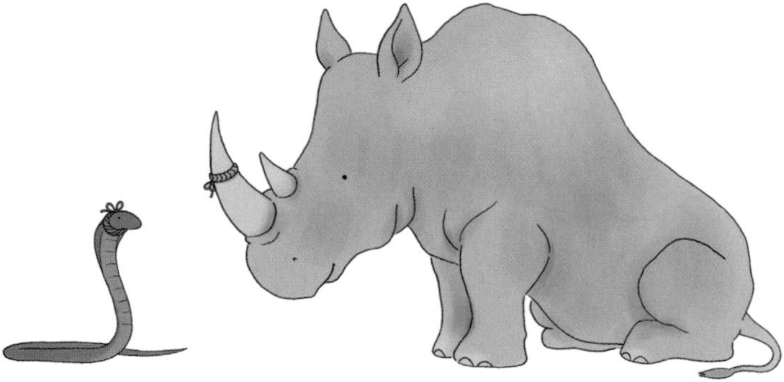

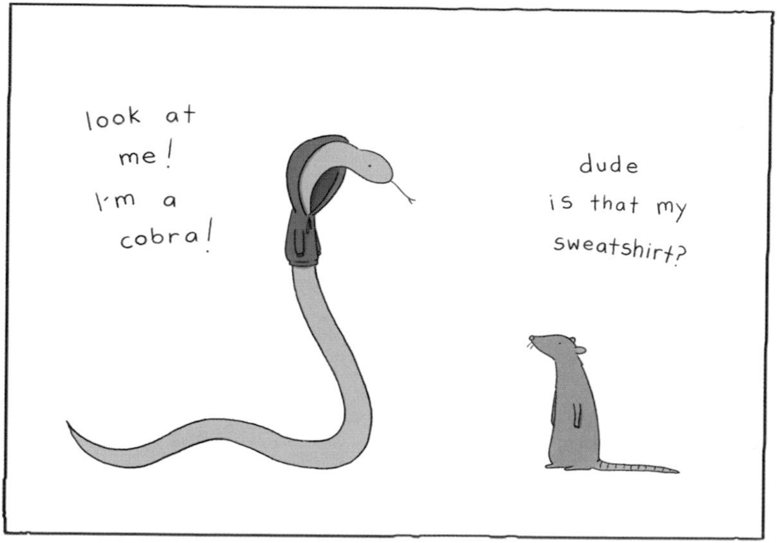
look at me! I'm a cobra!
dude is that my sweatshirt?

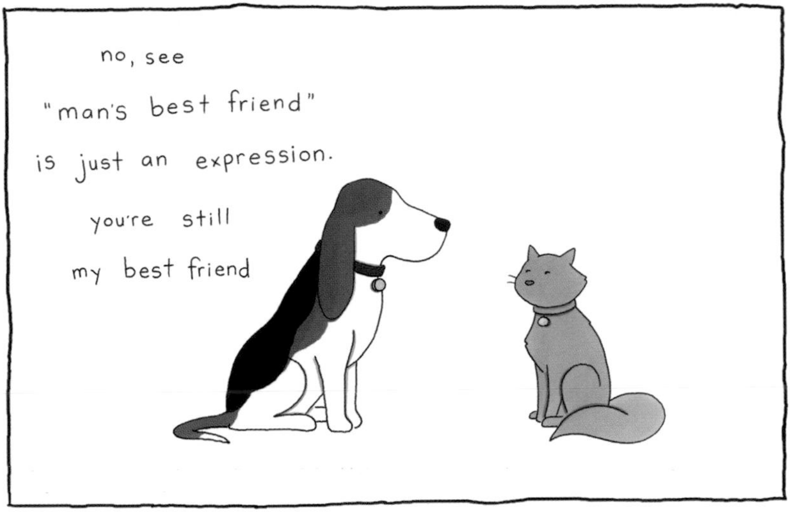
no, see
"man's best friend"
is just an expression.
you're still
my best friend

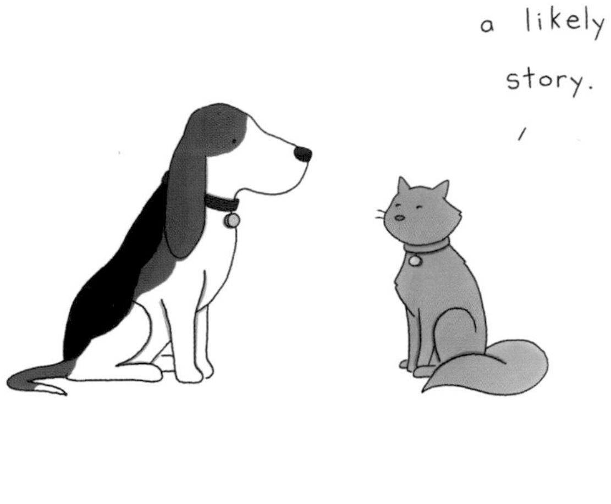
a likely
story.

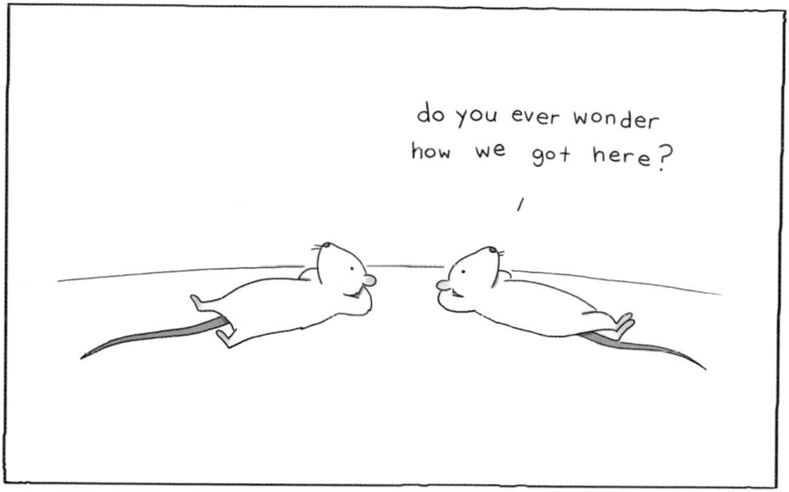
do you ever wonder
how we got here?

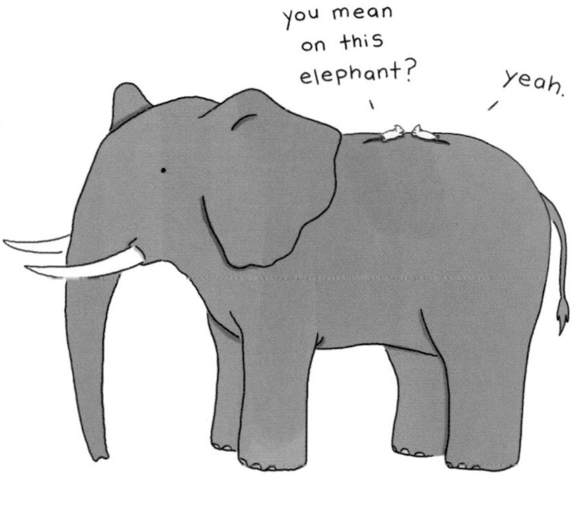
you mean
on this
elephant?
yeah.

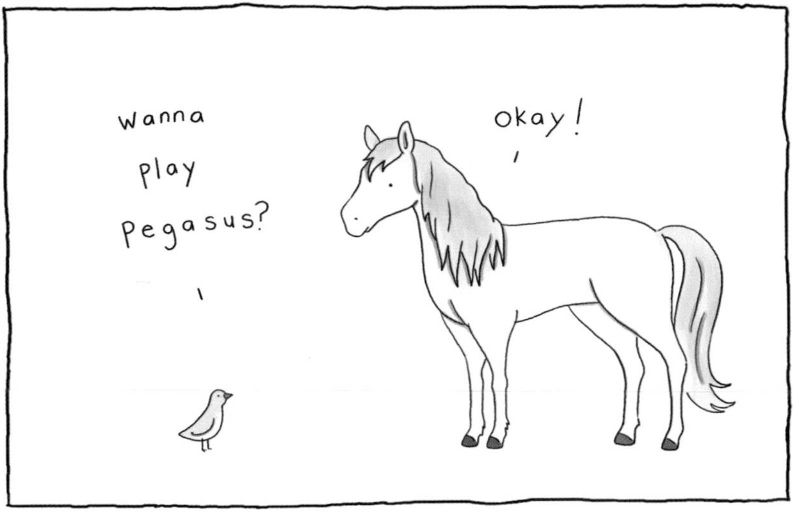
Wanna play Pegasus?
Okay!

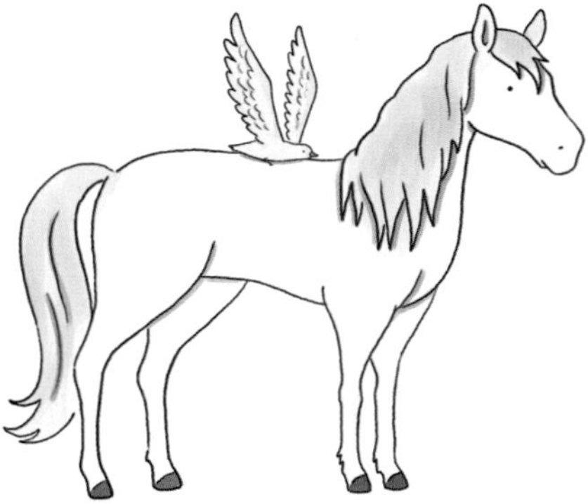

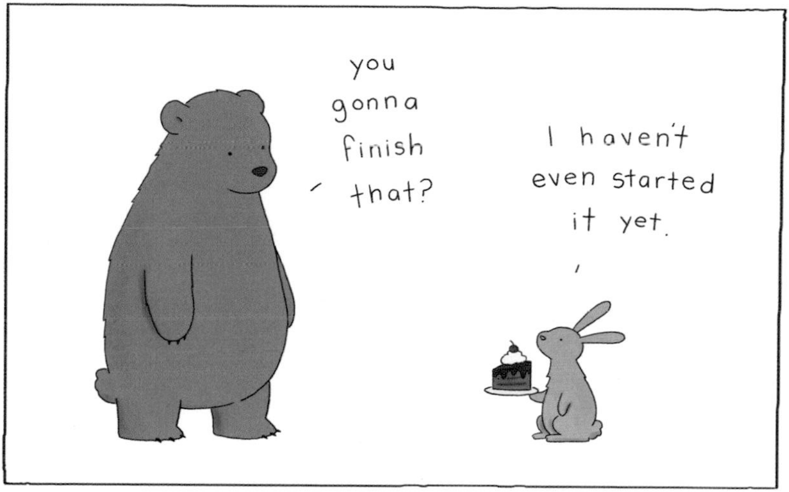
you gonna finish that?
I haven't even started it yet.

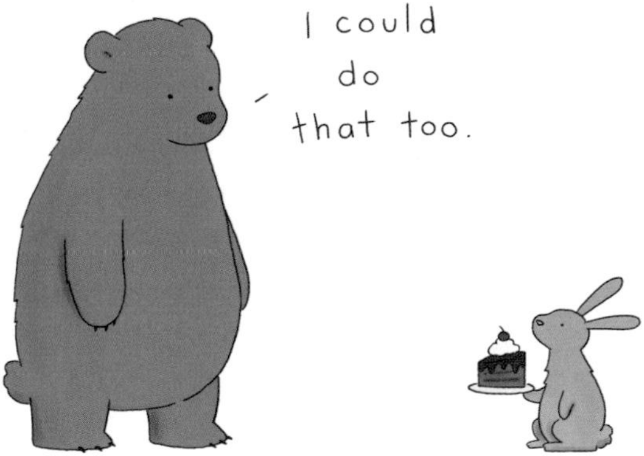
I could do that too.

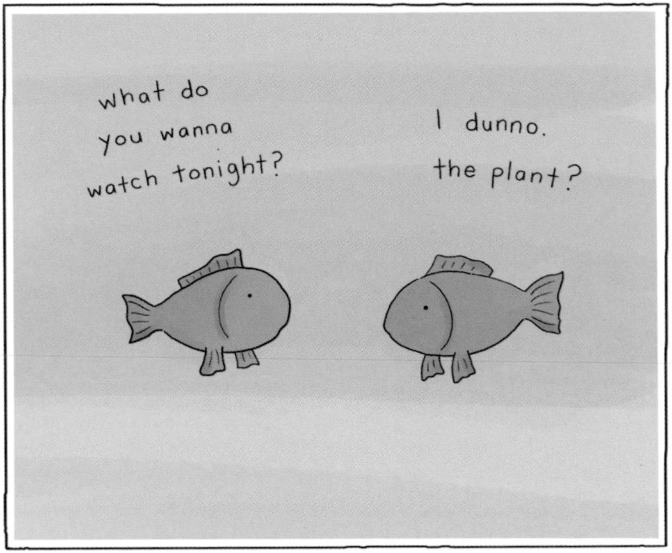
what do you wanna watch tonight?
I dunno. the plant?

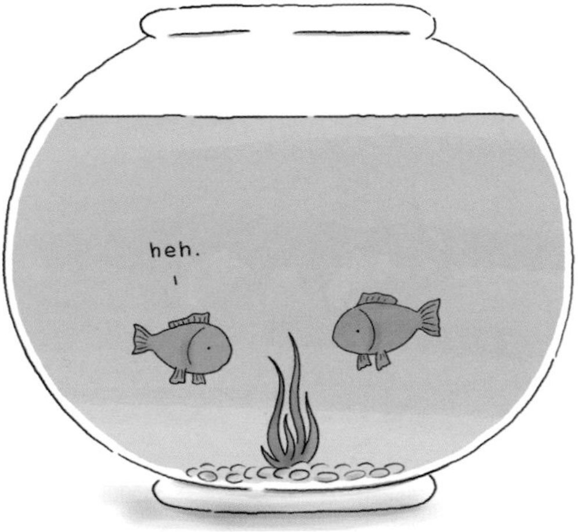
heh.

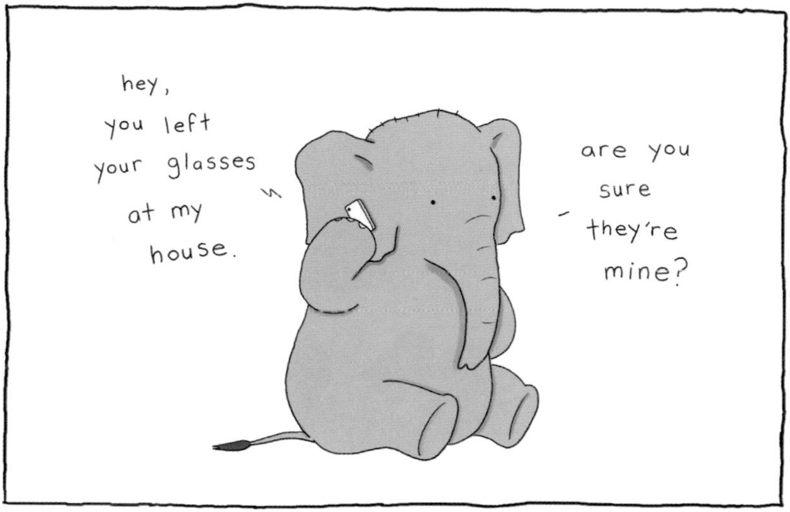
hey, you left your glasses at my house.
are you sure they're mine?

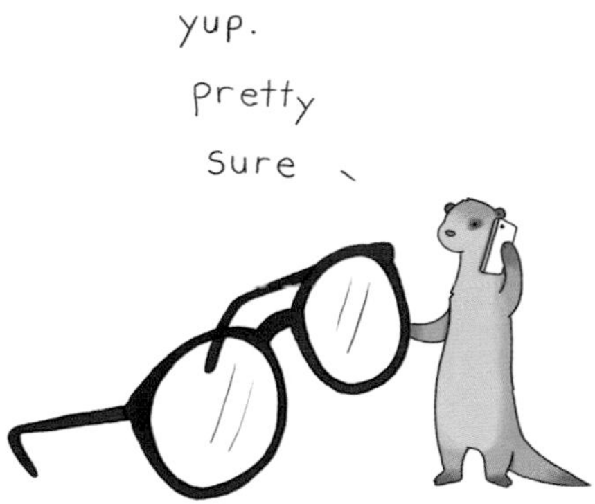
yup. pretty sure

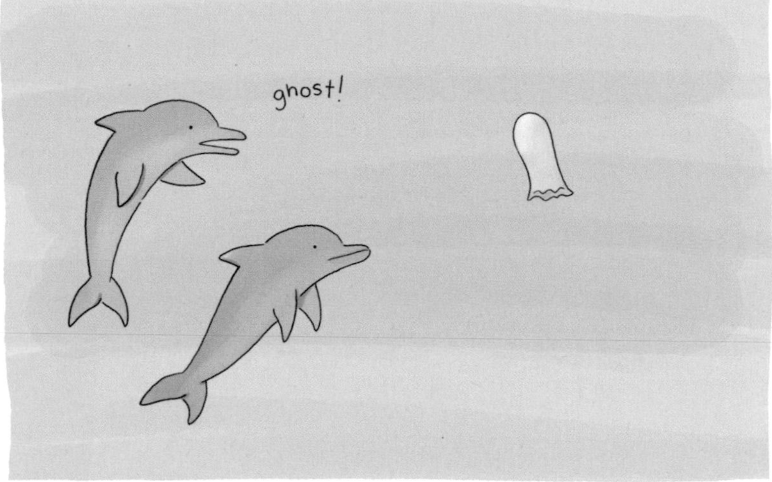
ghost!

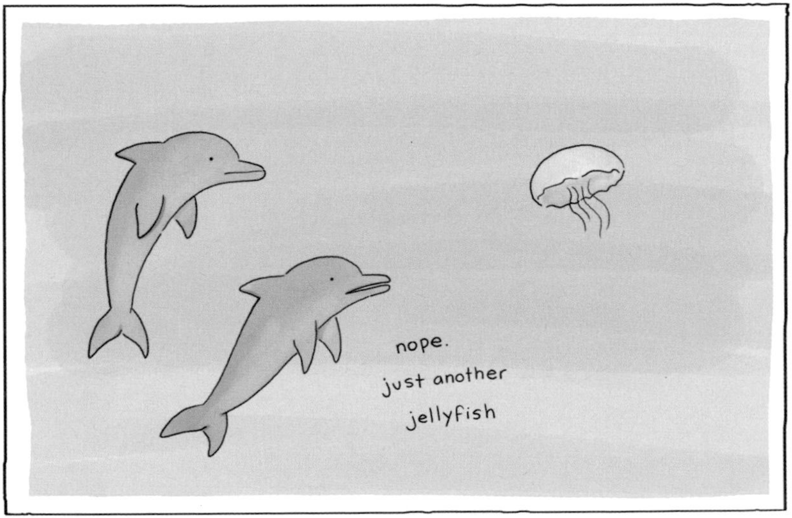
nope.
just another
jellyfish

dude!

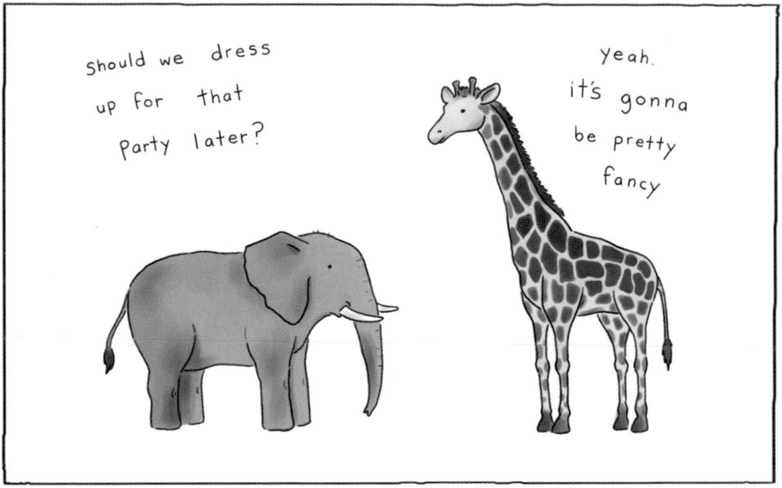
should we dress up for that party later?
yeah. it's gonna be pretty fancy

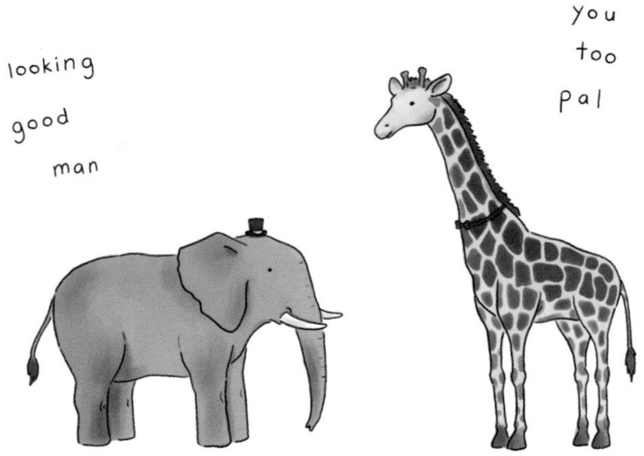
looking good man
you too pal

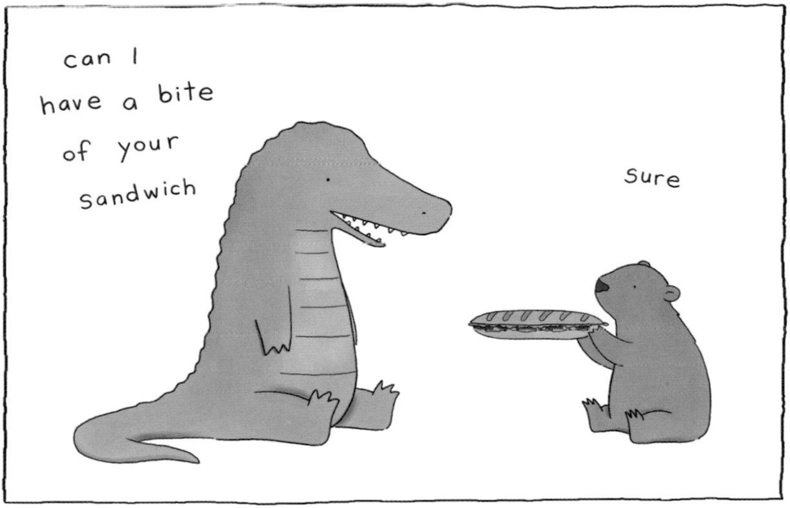
can I
have a bite
of your
sandwich
sure

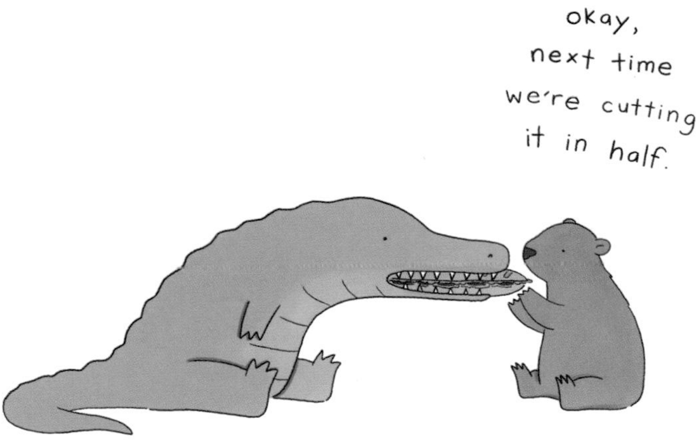
okay,
next time
we're cutting
it in half.

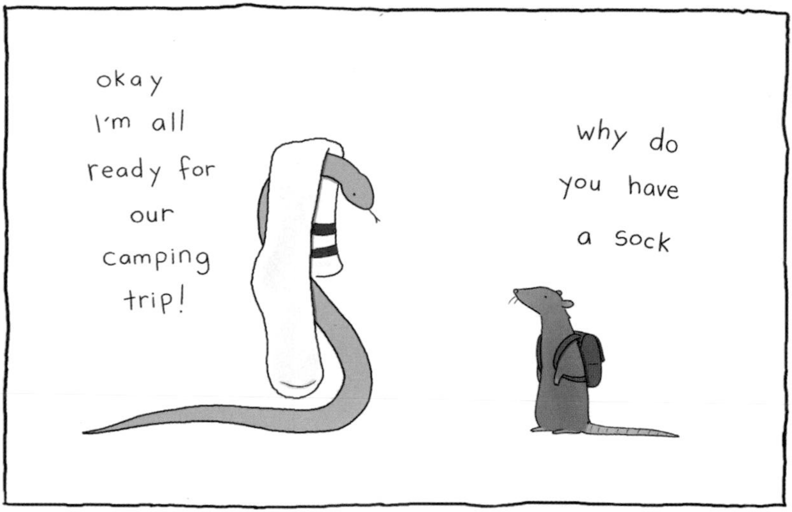
okay I'm all ready for our camping trip!
why do you have a sock

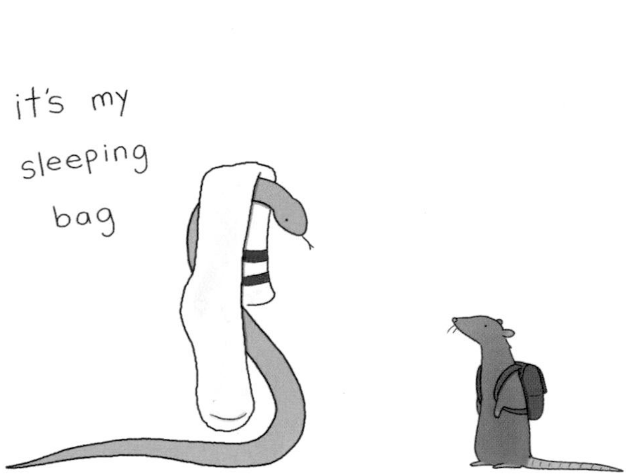
it's my sleeping bag

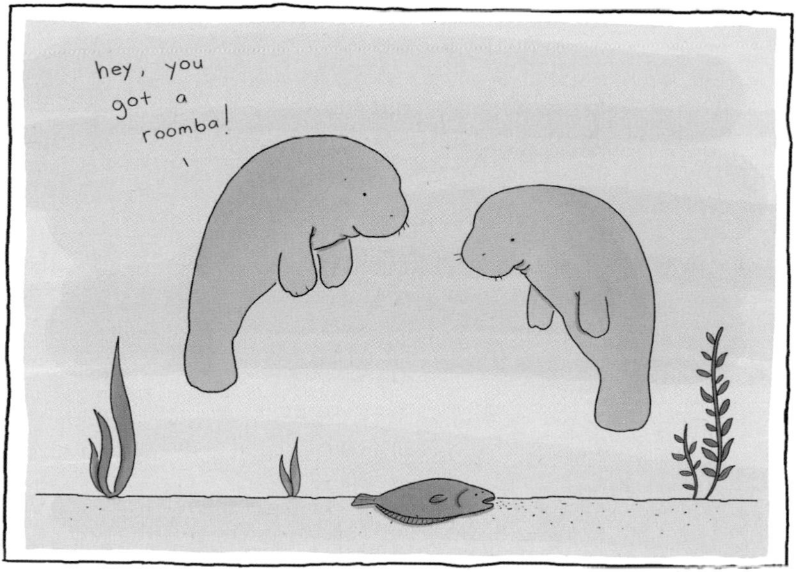
hey, you
got a
roomba!

hanging
out

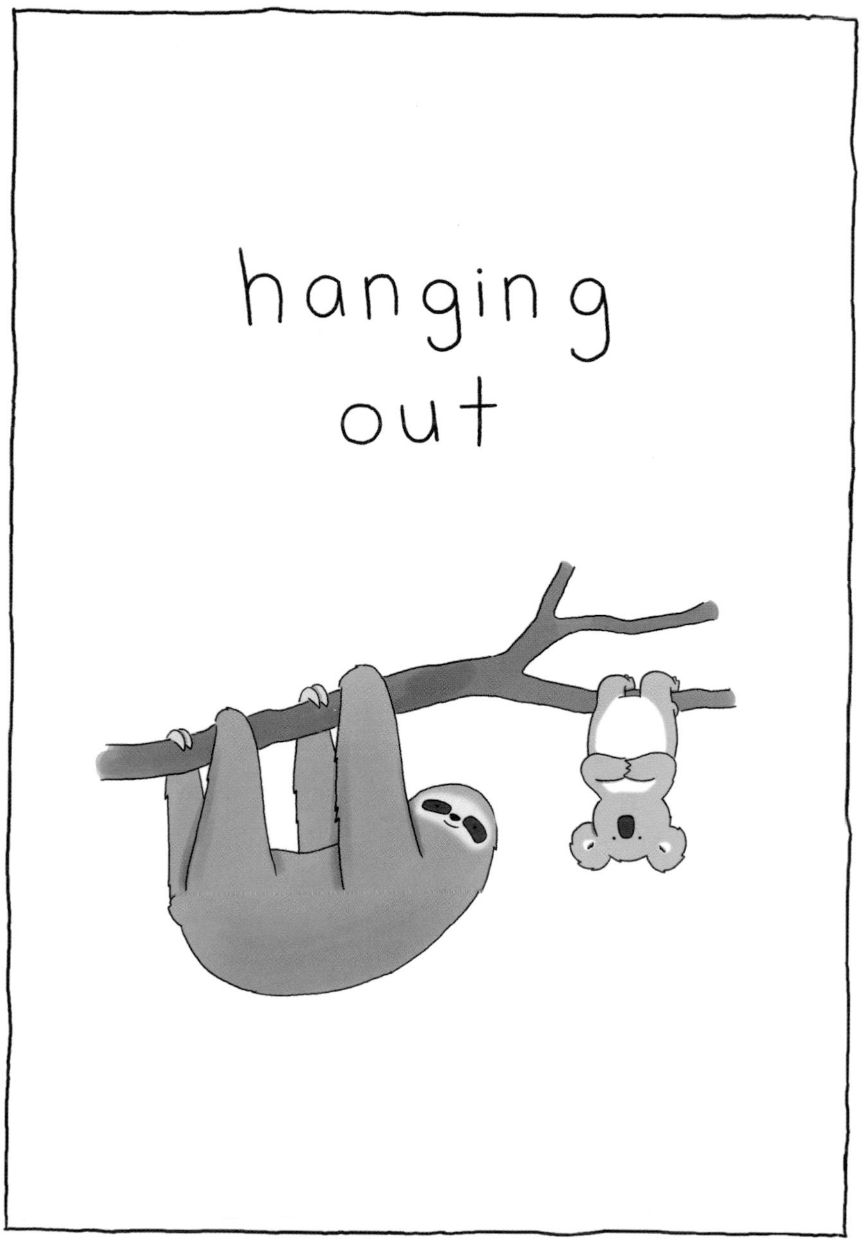

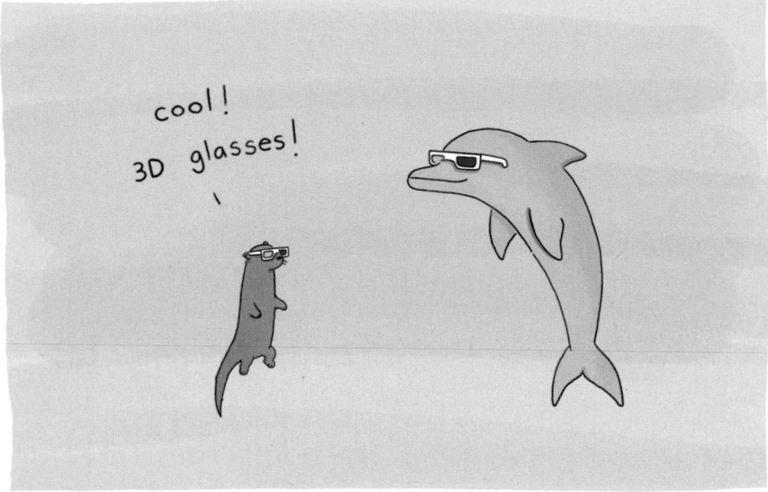
cool!
3D glasses!

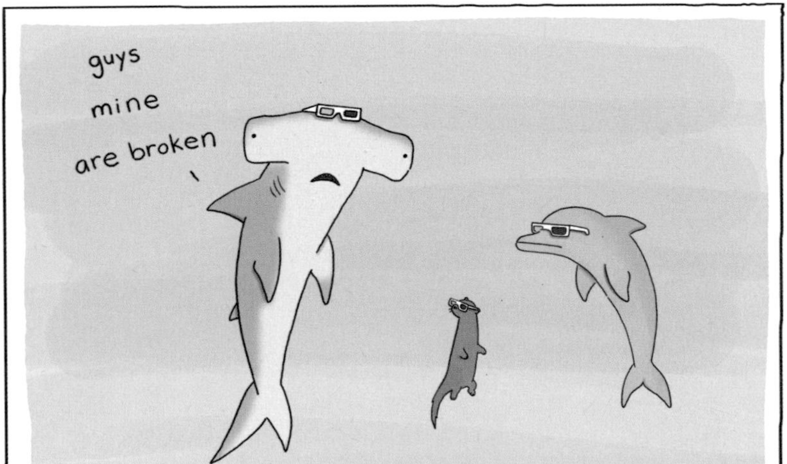
guys
mine
are broken

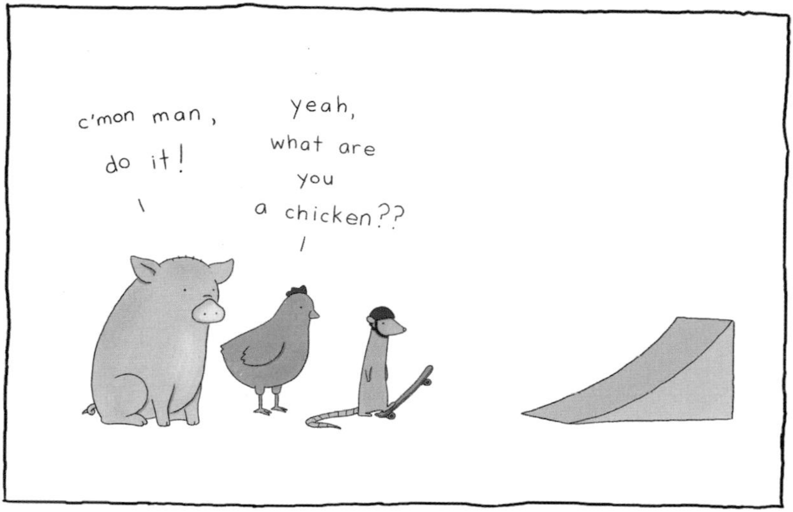
c'mon man, do it!
yeah, what are you a chicken??

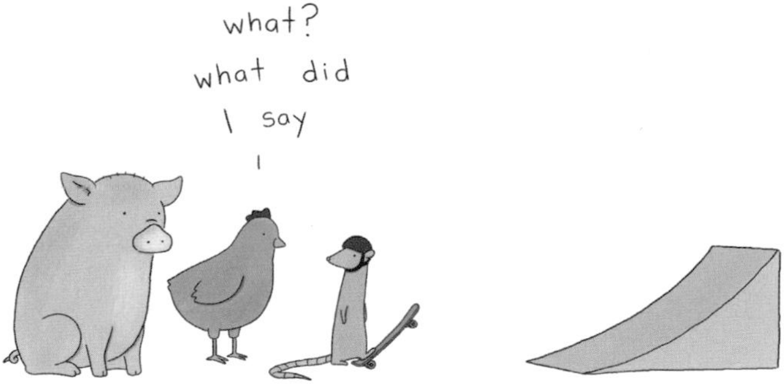
what? what did I say

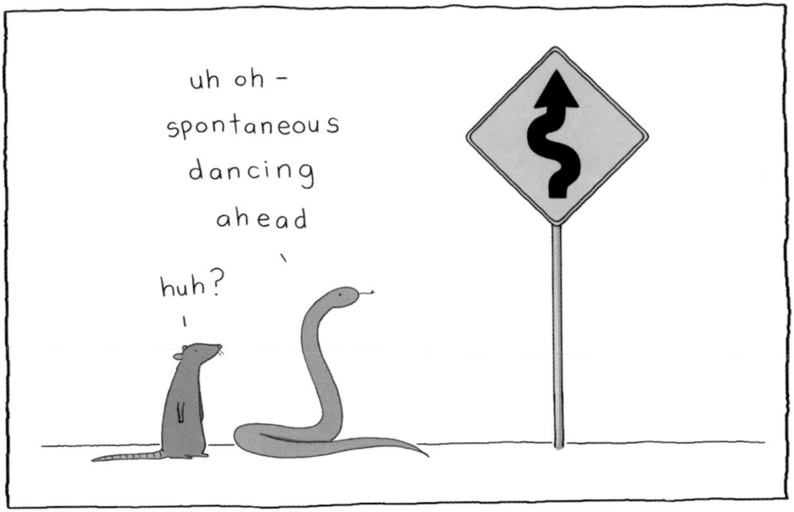
uh oh - spontaneous dancing ahead
huh?

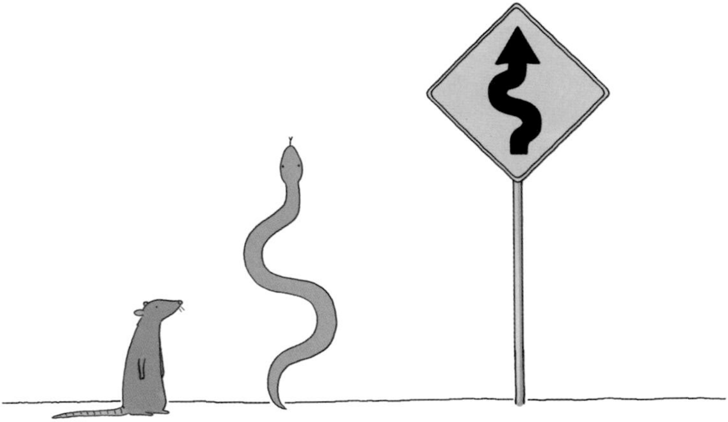

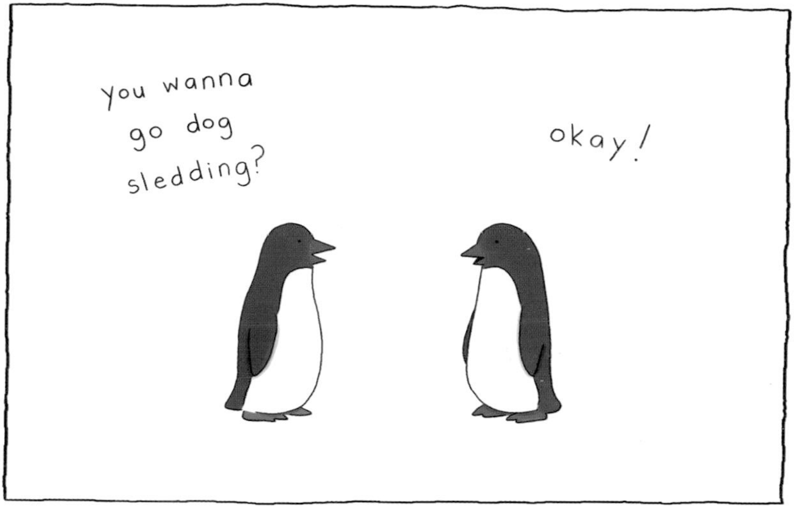
you wanna go dog sledding?
okay!

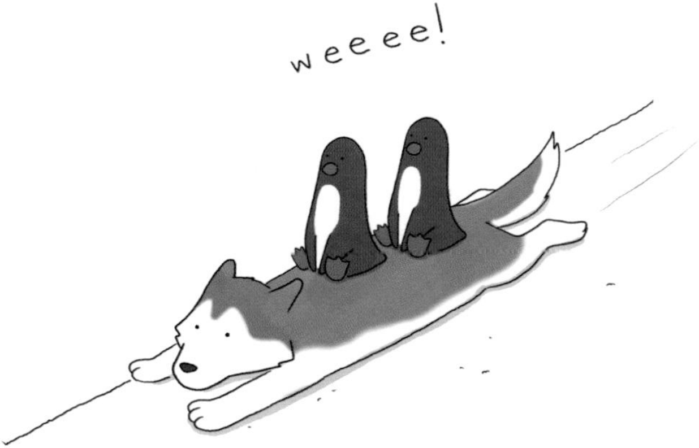
weeee!

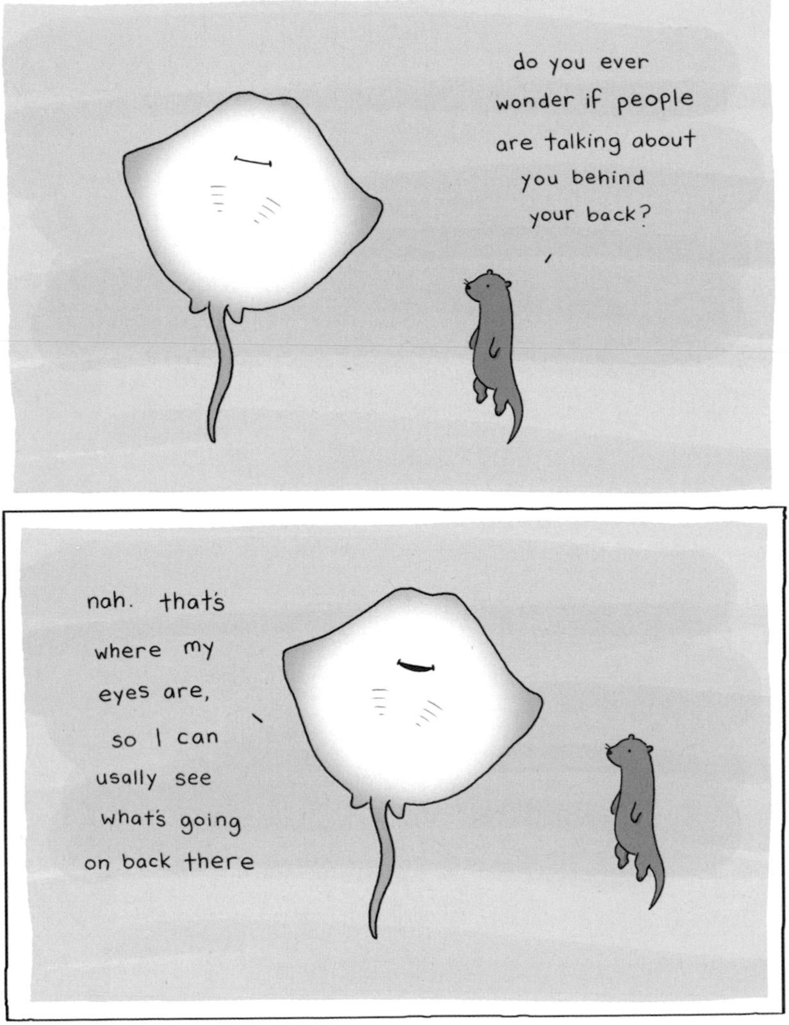
do you ever wonder if people are talking about you behind your back?
nah. that's where my eyes are, so I can usally see what's going on back there

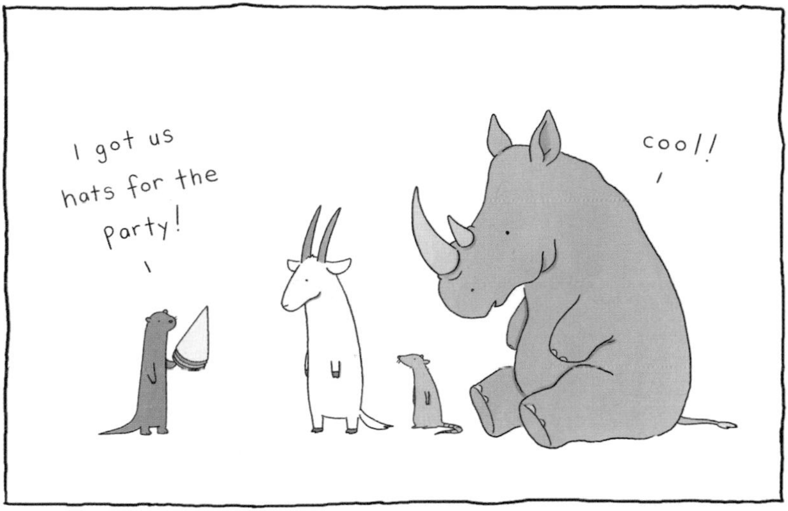
I got us hats for the party!
cool!!

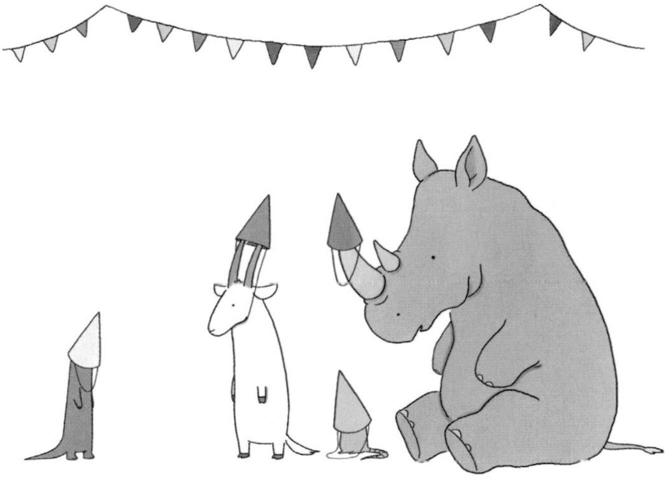

wow, your hair looks amazing! what kind of shampoo do you use?

flea and tick

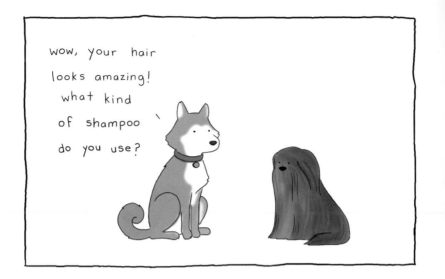

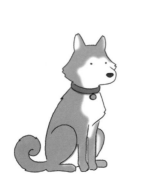

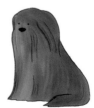

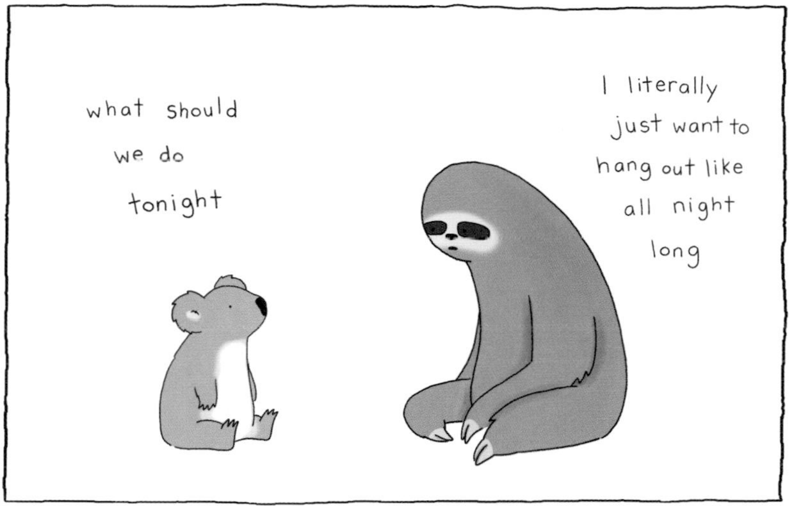
what should
we do
tonight
I literally
just want to
hang out like
all night
long

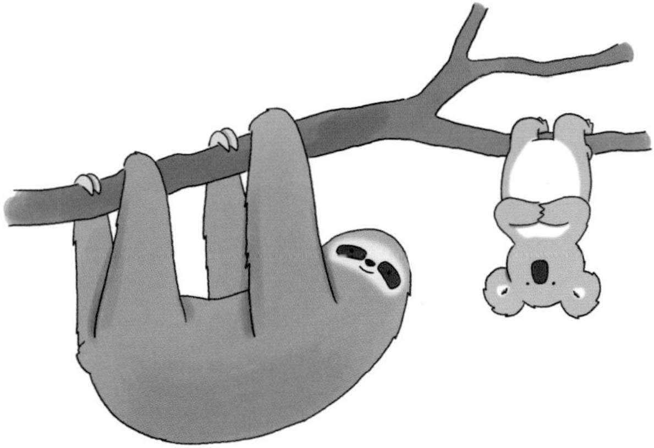

hey man wanna play?
so that's where all my shoes went

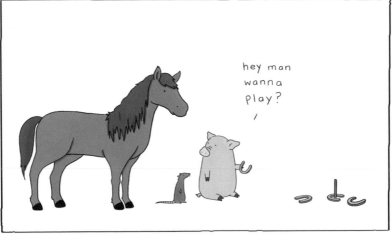

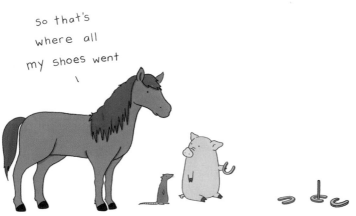

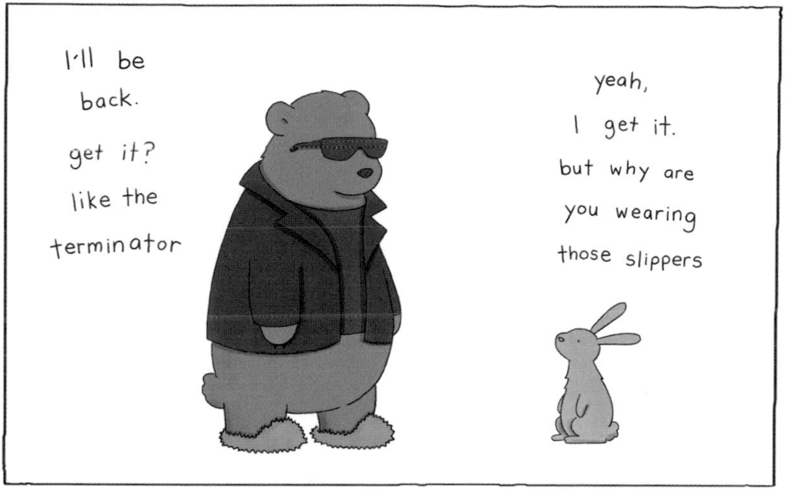
I'll be back.
get it?
like the terminator
yeah,
I get it.
but why are you wearing those slippers

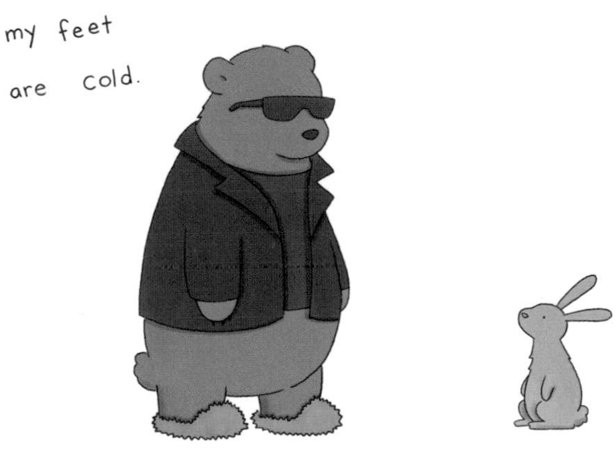
my feet are cold.

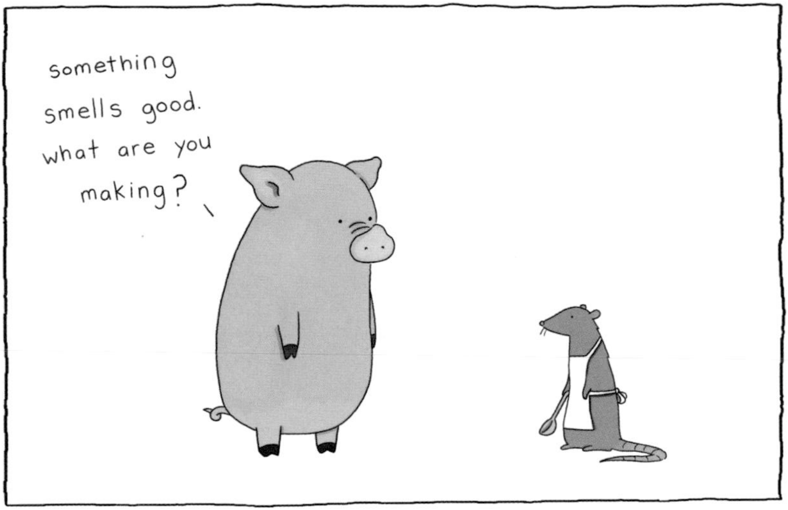
something smells good. what are you making?

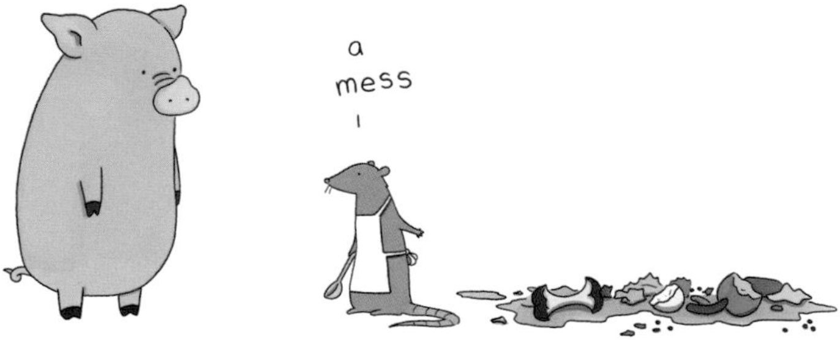
a mess

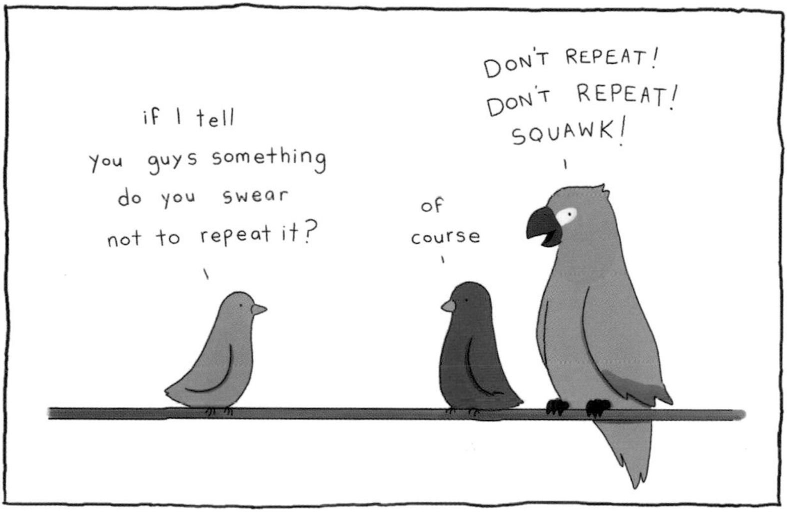
if I tell you guys something do you swear not to repeat it?
of course
DON'T REPEAT! DON'T REPEAT! SQUAWK!

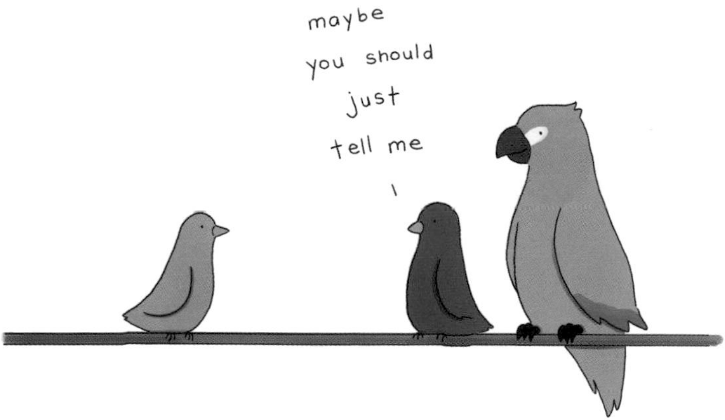
maybe you should just tell me

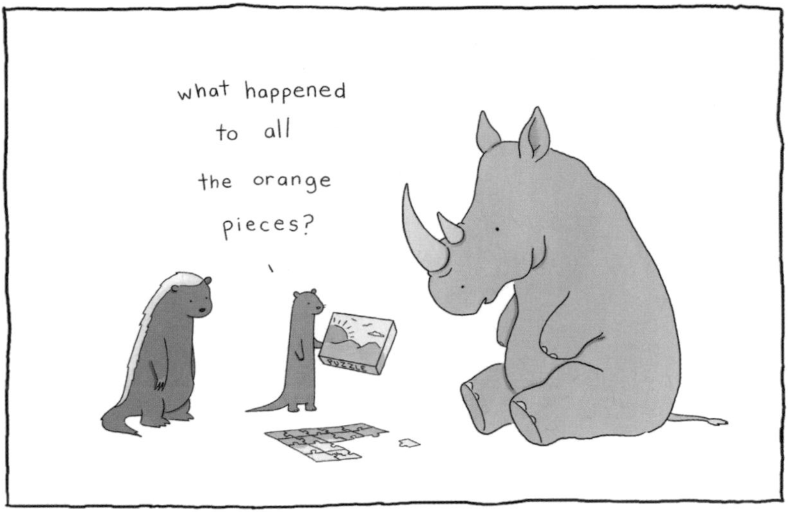
what happened to all the orange pieces?
PUZZLE

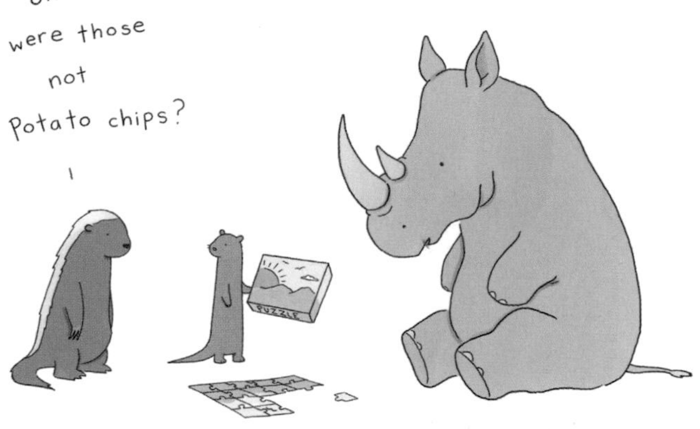
oh were those not potato chips?
PUZZLE

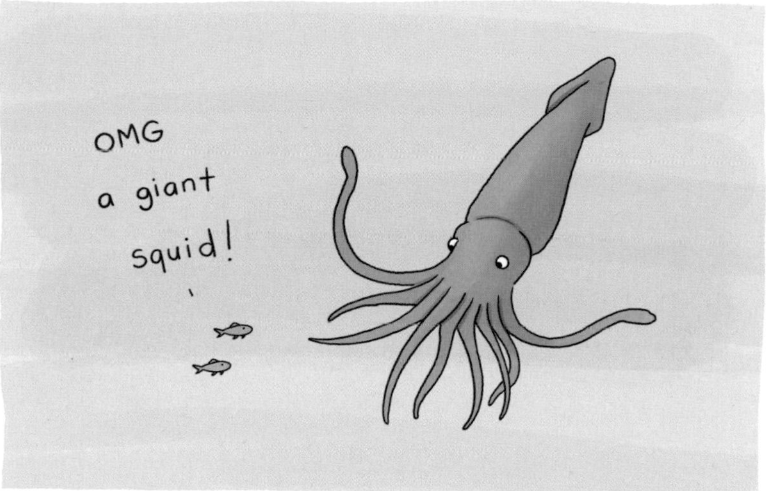
OMG
a giant
squid!

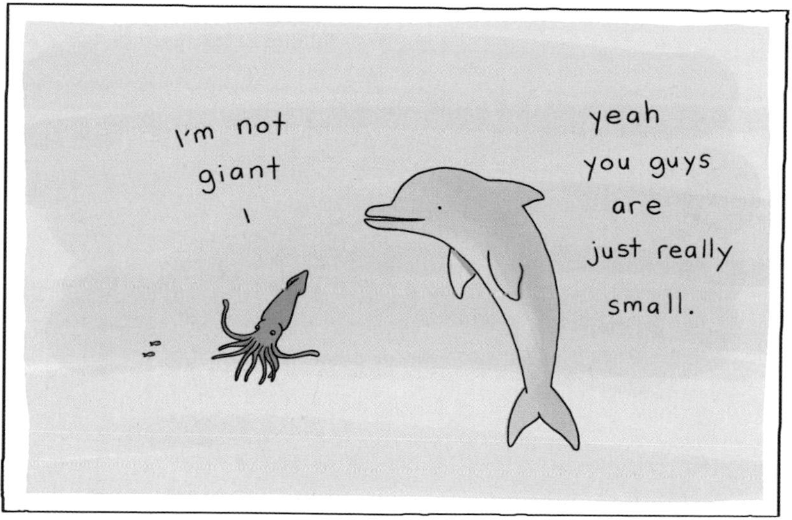
I'm not
giant
yeah
you guys
are
just really
small.

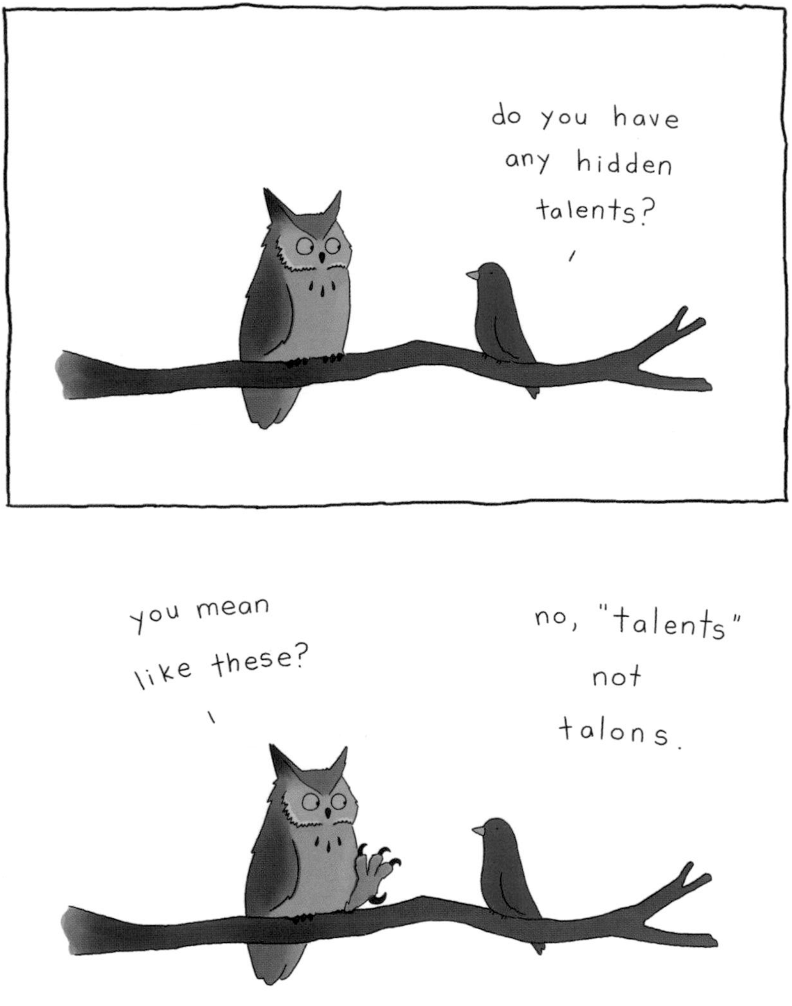
do you have any hidden talents?
you mean like these?
no, "talents" not talons.

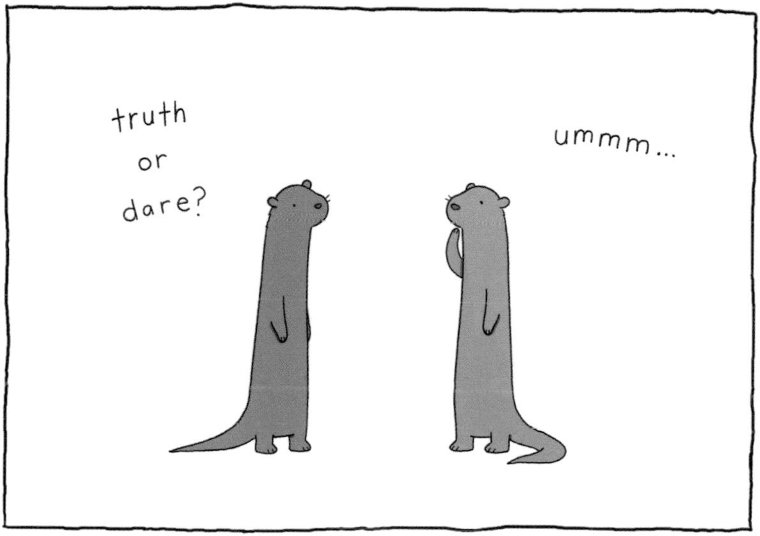
truth or dare?
ummm...

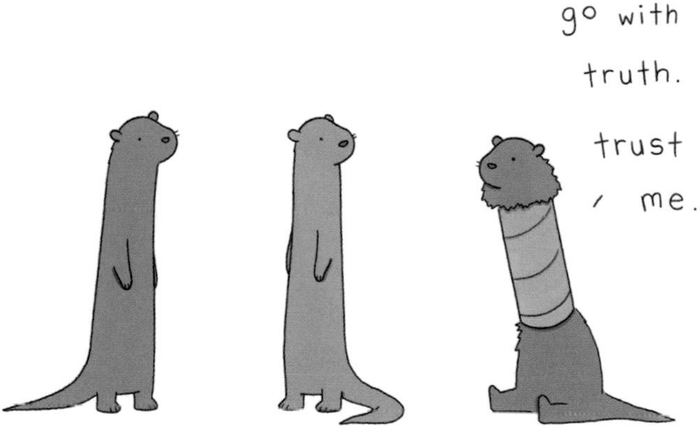
go with truth. trust me.

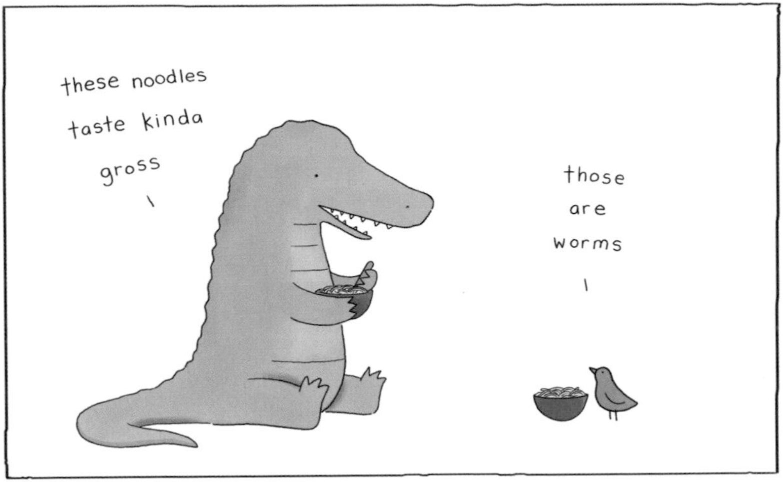
these noodles taste kinda gross
those are worms

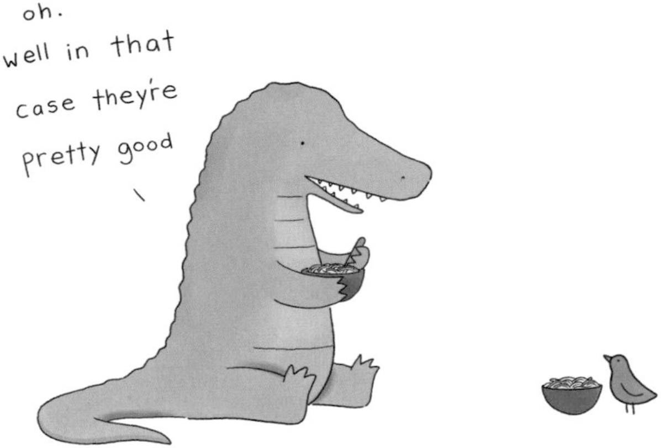
oh.
well in that case they're pretty good

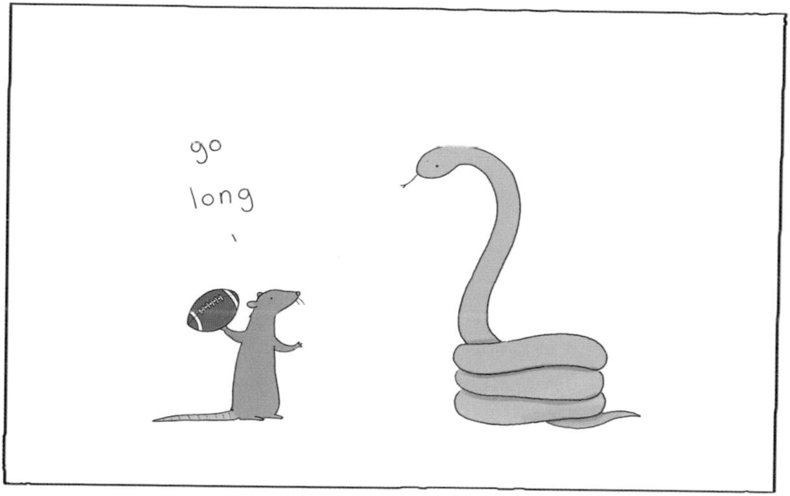
go
long

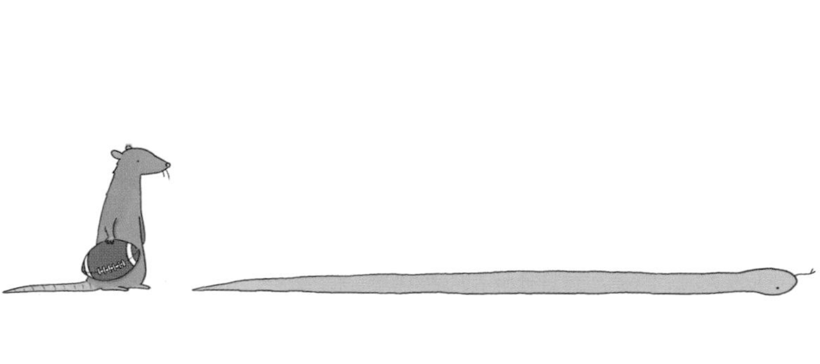

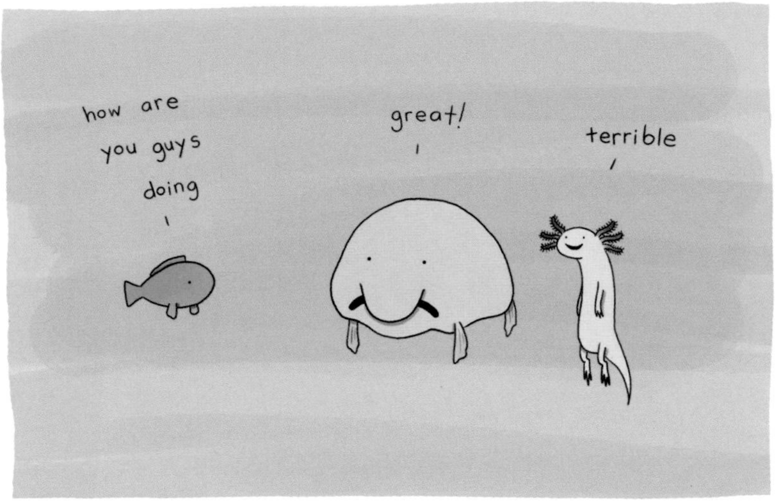
how are you guys doing
great!
terrible

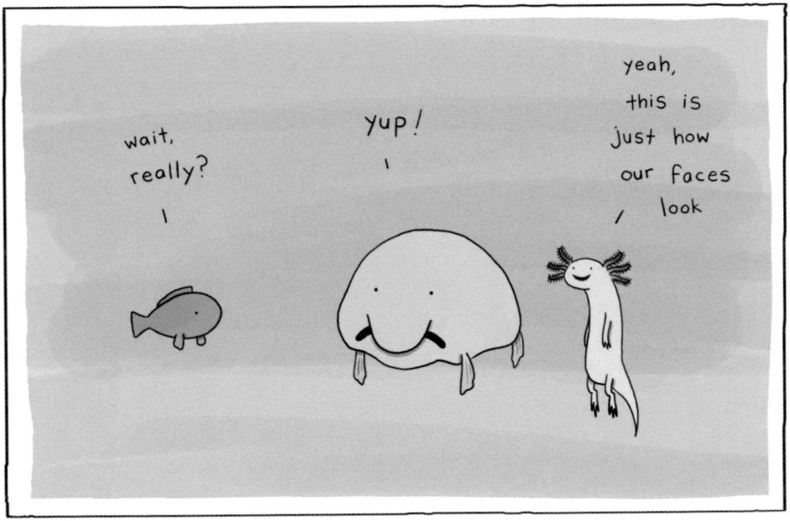
wait, really?
yup!
yeah, this is just how our faces look

Painting
easter eggs
is fun!

dude
that's my
brother.

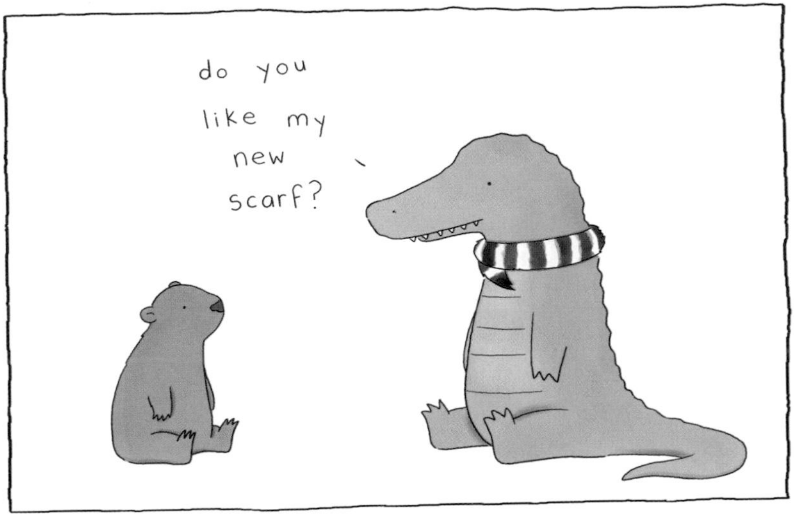
do you like my new scarf?

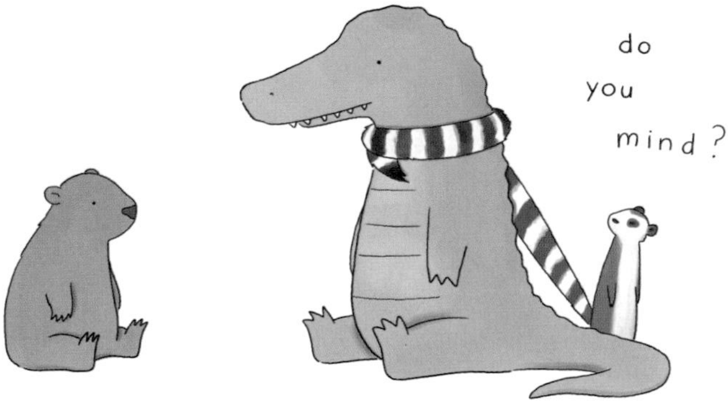
do you mind?

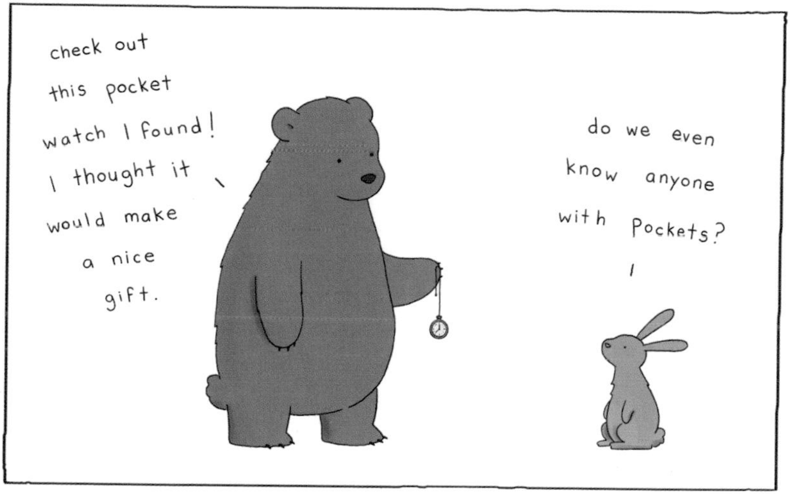
check out this pocket watch I found! I thought it would make a nice gift.
do we even know anyone with Pockets?

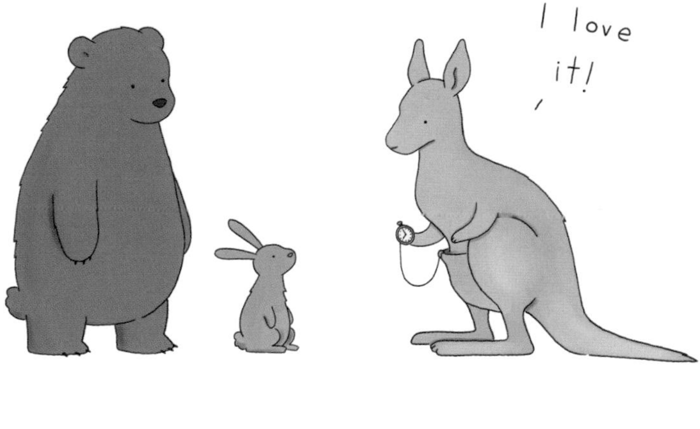
I love it!

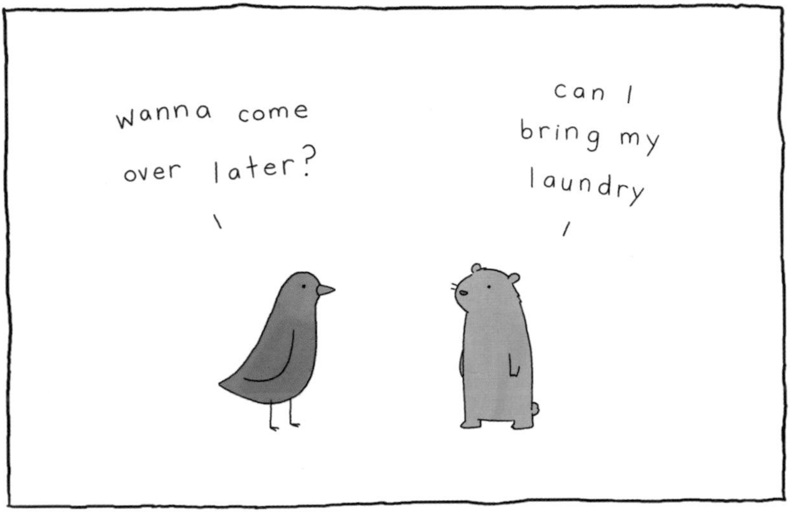
wanna come over later?
can I bring my laundry

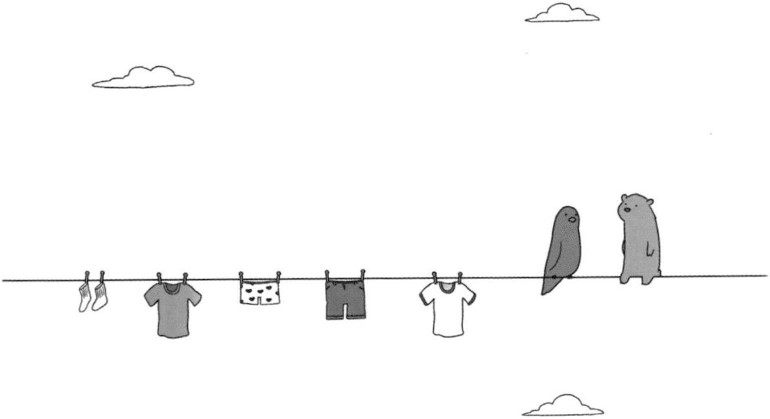

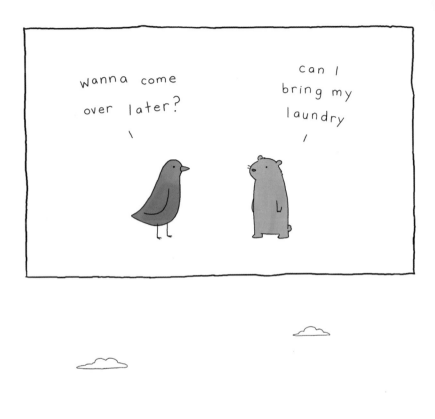

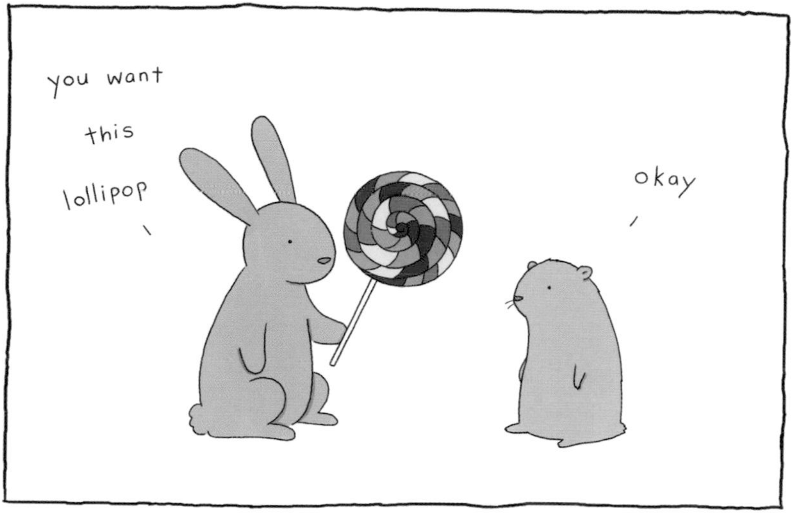
you want this lollipop
okay

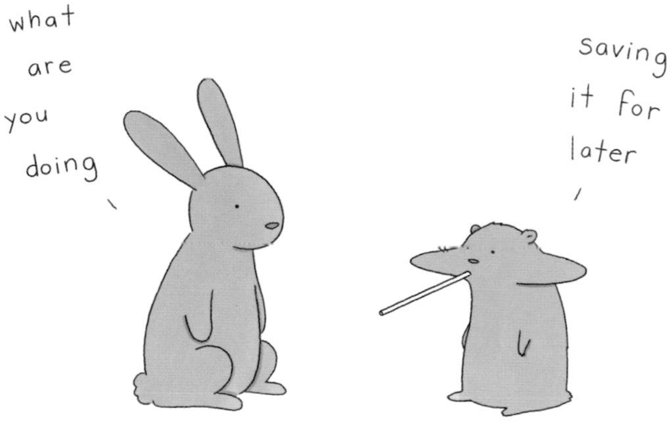
what are you doing
saving it for later

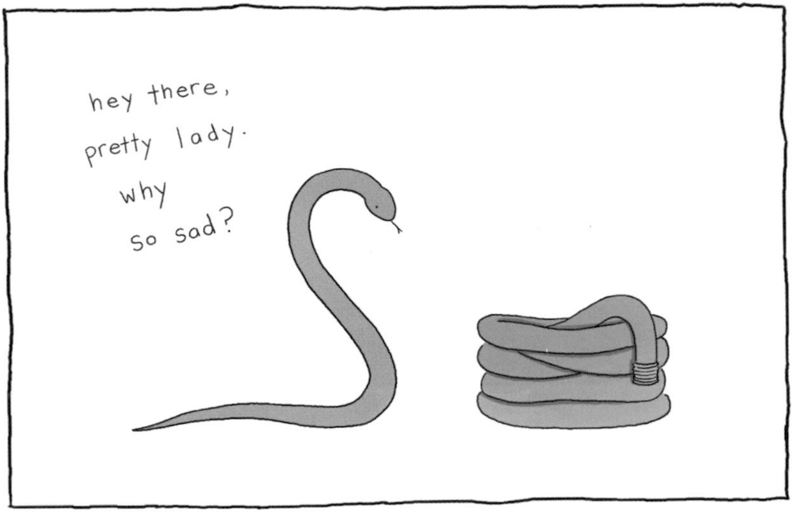
hey there,
pretty lady.
why
so sad?

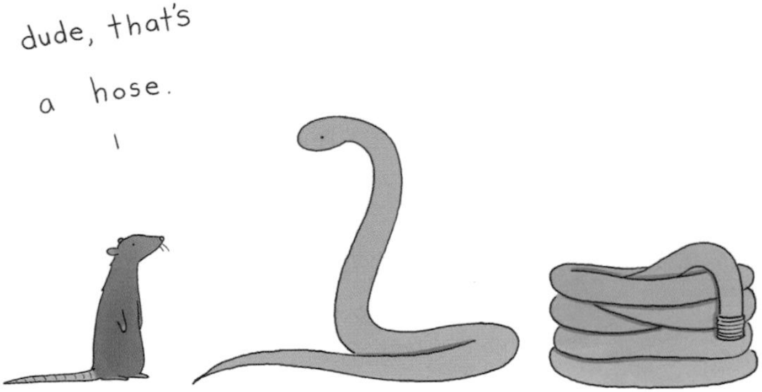
dude, that's
a hose.

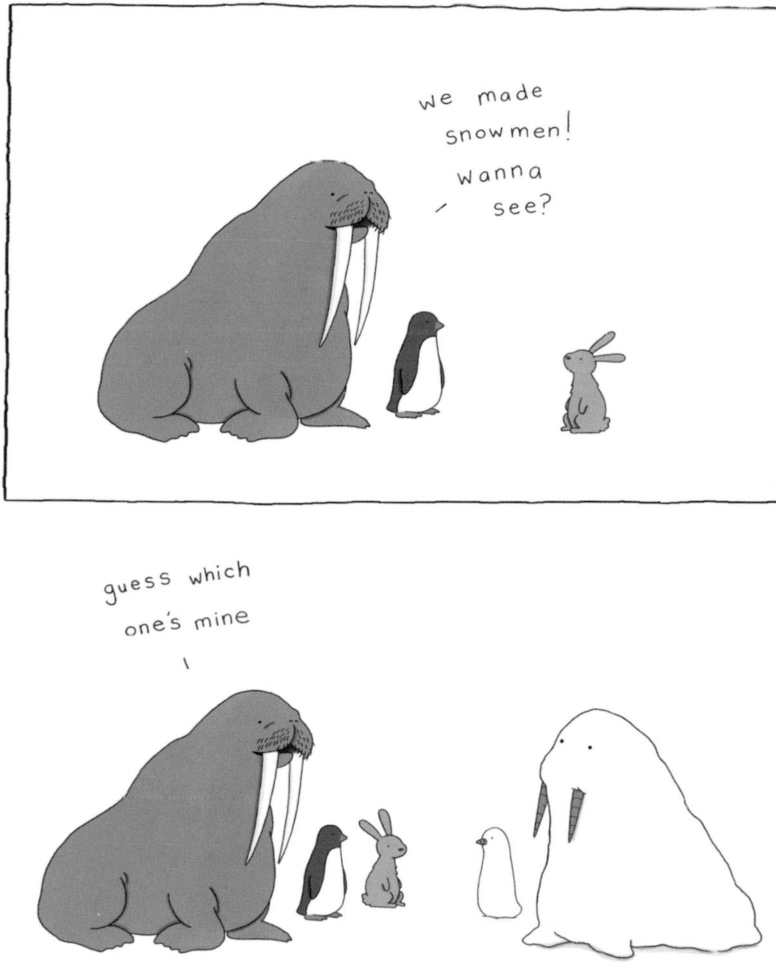
we made snowmen! wanna see?
guess which one's mine

unlikely
friends

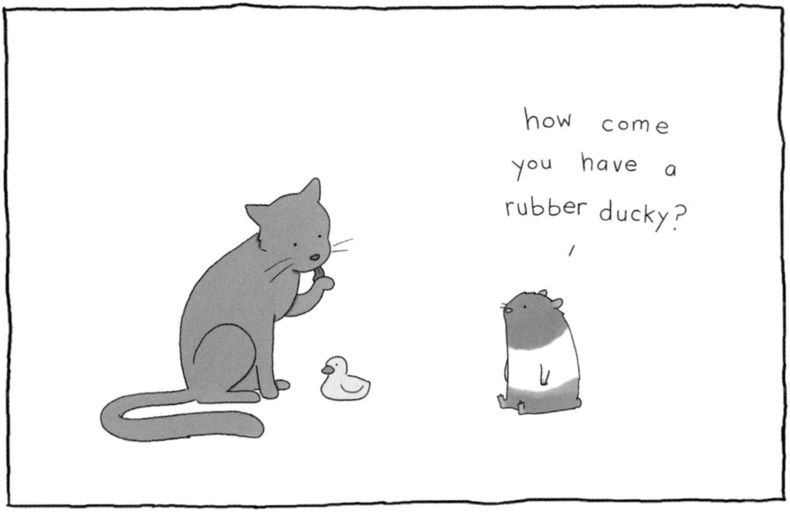
how come you have a rubber ducky?

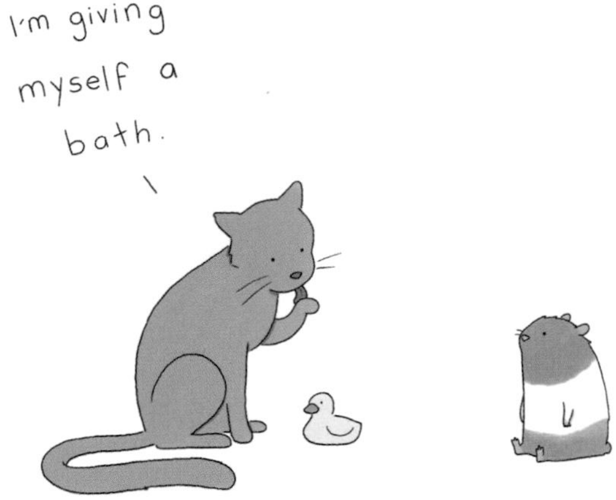
I'm giving myself a bath.

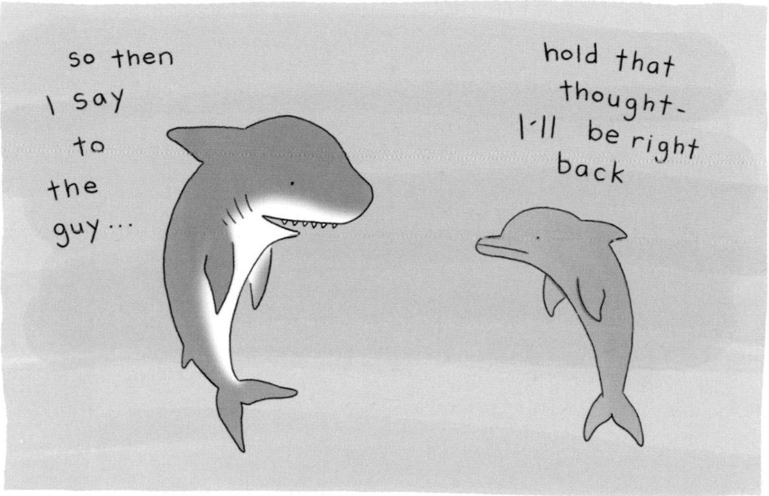
so then I say to the guy...
hold that thought- I'll be right back

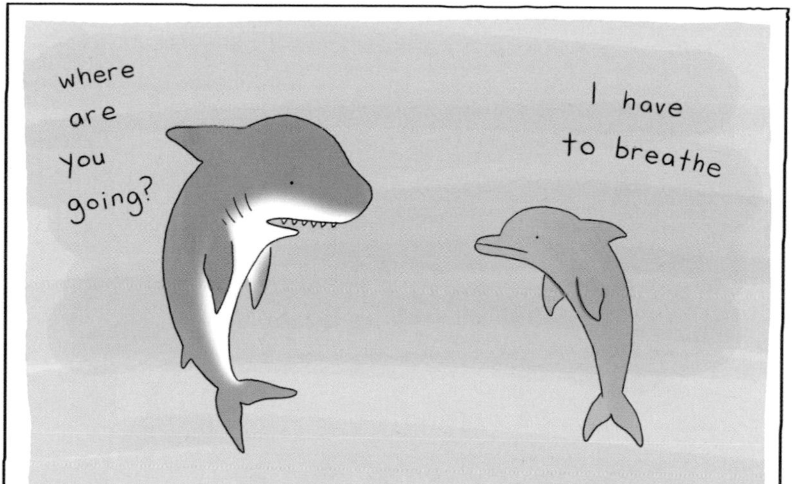
where are you going?
I have to breathe

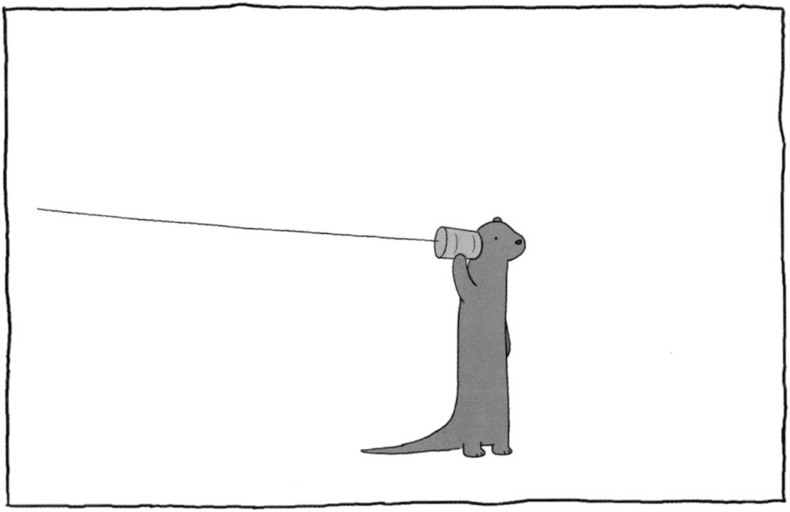

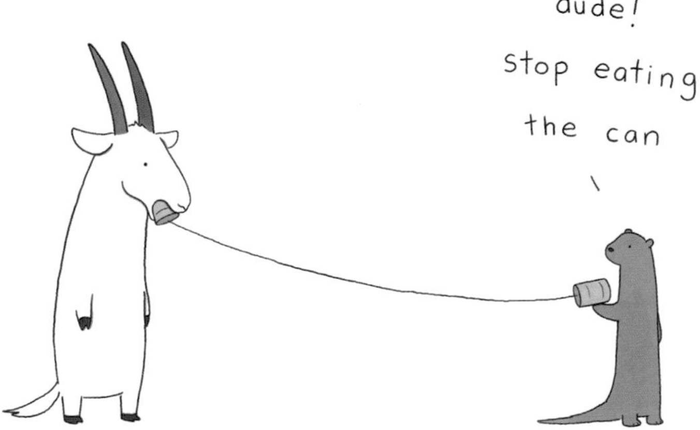
dude! stop eating the can

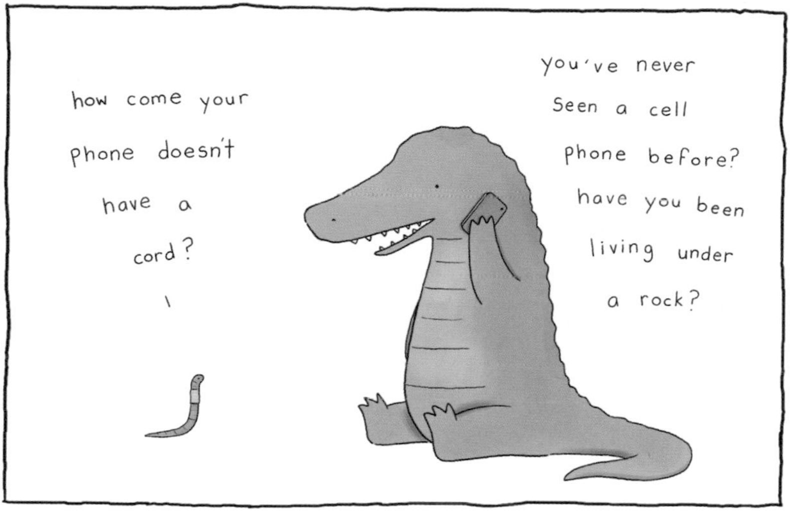
how come your phone doesn't have a cord?
you've never seen a cell phone before? have you been living under a rock?

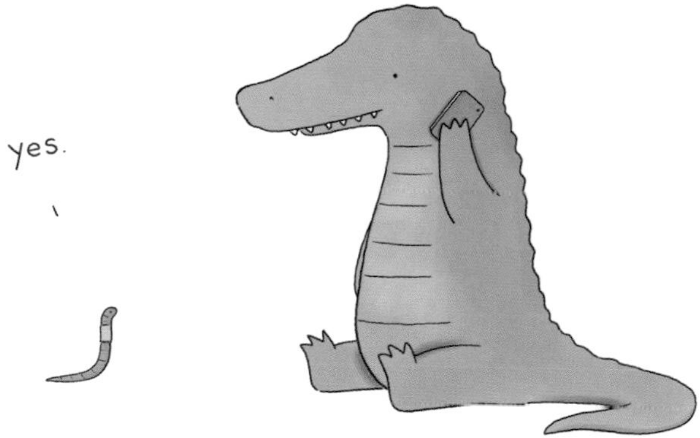
yes.

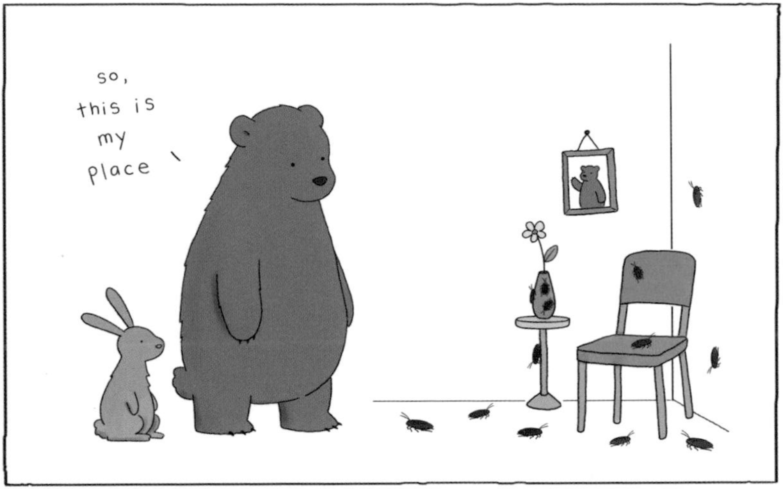
so, this is my place

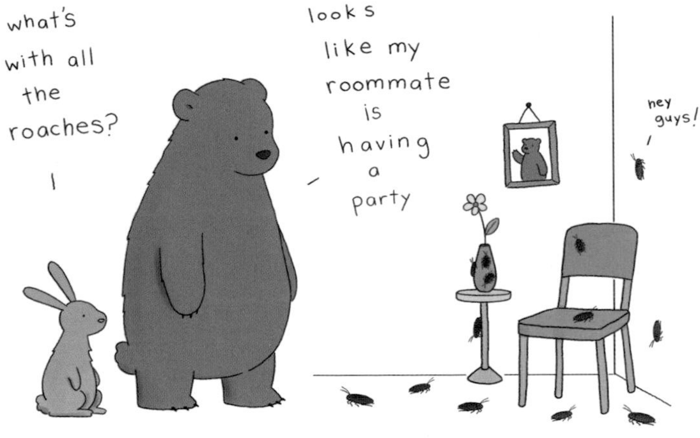
what's with all the roaches?
looks like my roommate is having a party
hey guys!

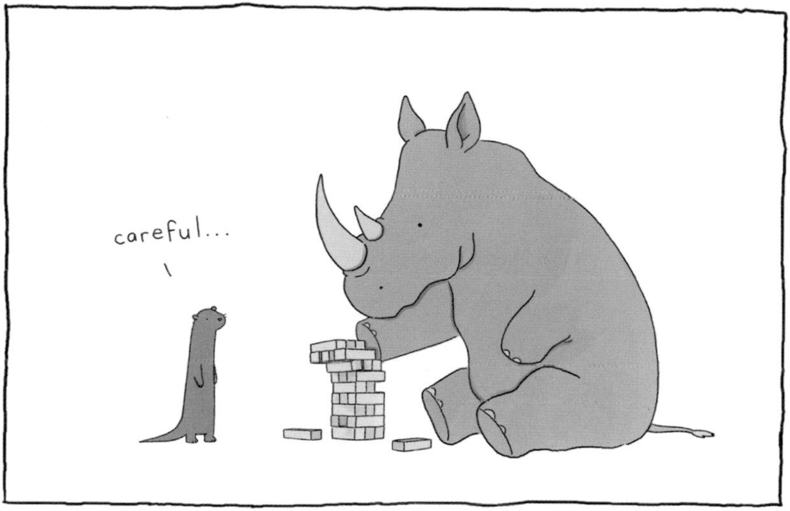
careful...

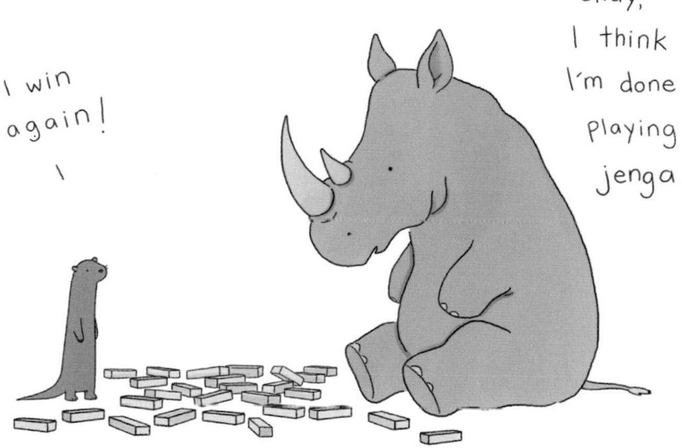
I win again!
okay, I think I'm done playing jenga.

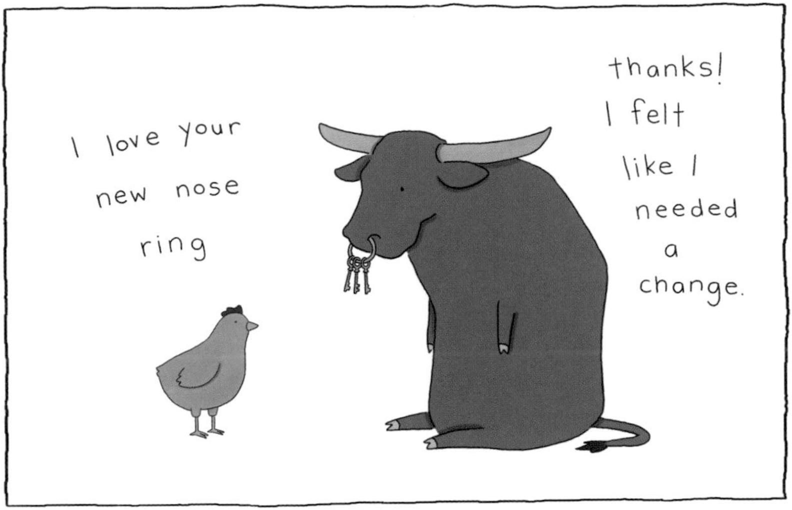
I love your new nose ring
thanks! I felt like I needed a change.

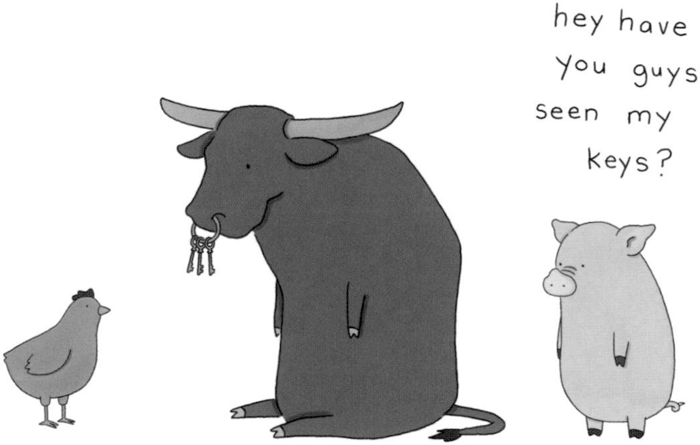
hey have you guys seen my keys?

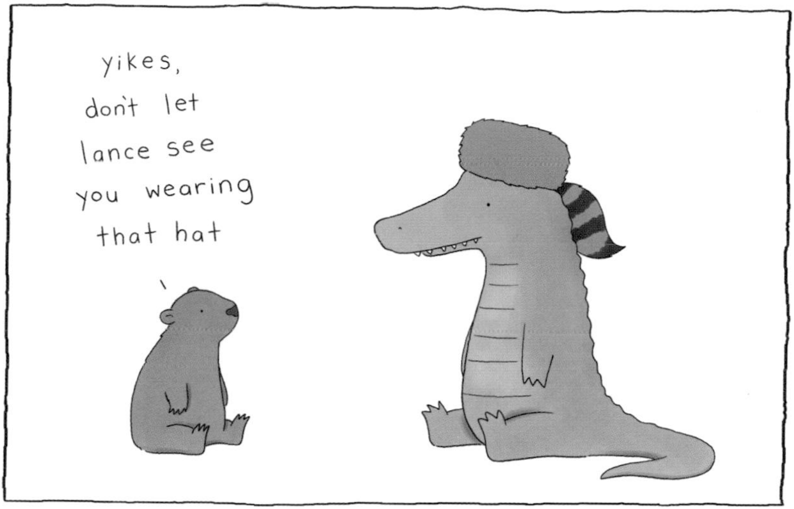
yikes, don't let lance see you wearing that hat

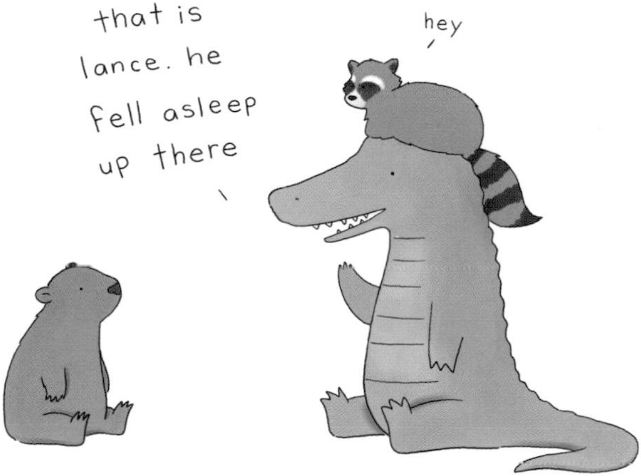
that is lance. he fell asleep up there
hey

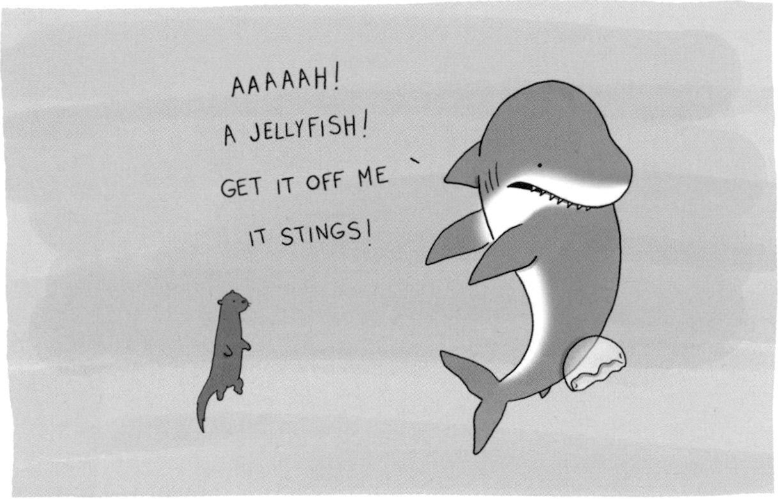
AAAAAH!
A JELLYFISH!
GET IT OFF ME
IT STINGS!

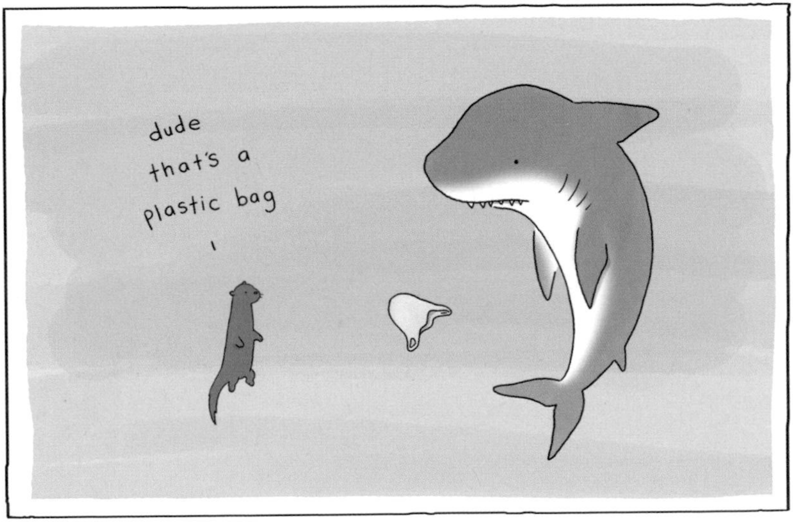
dude
that's a
plastic bag

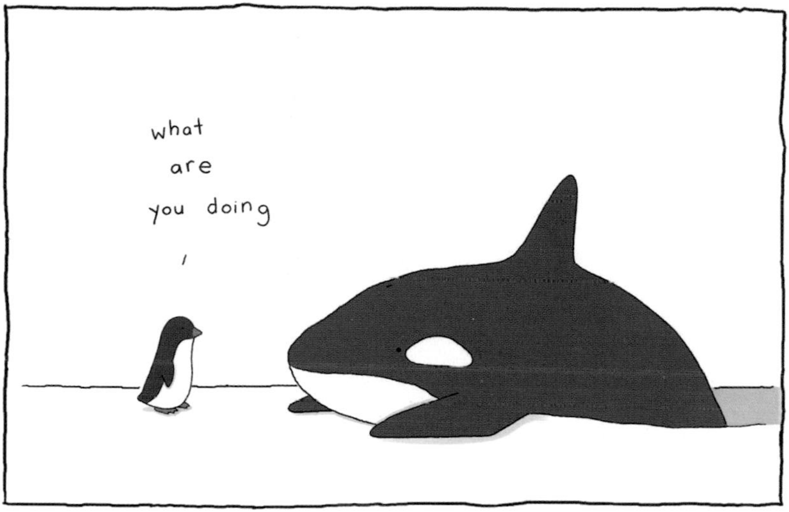
what are you doing

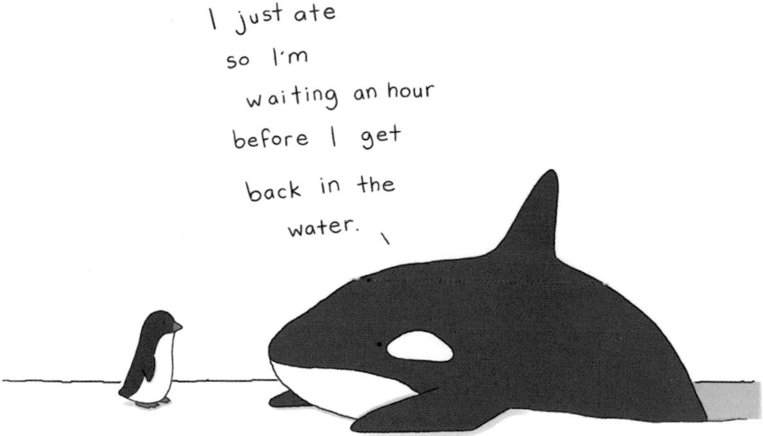
I just ate so I'm waiting an hour before I get back in the water.

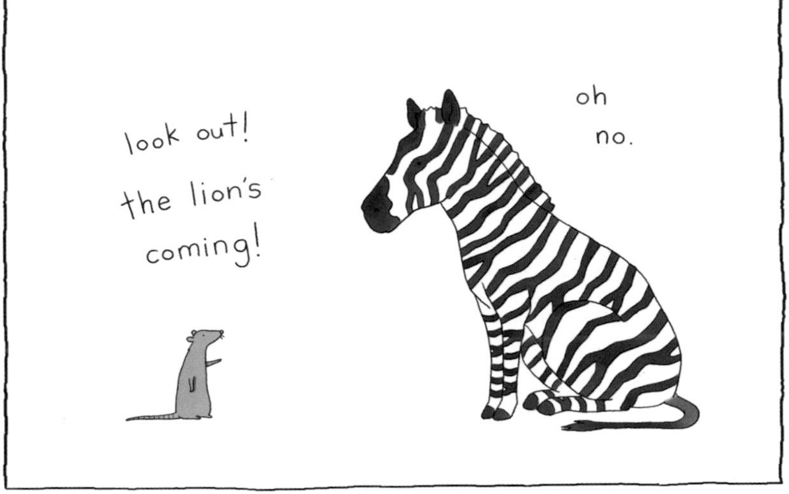
look out!
the lion's
coming!
oh
no.

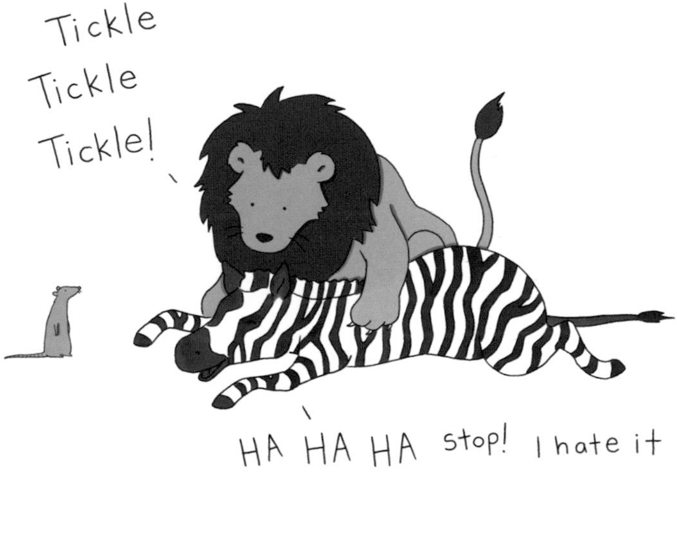
Tickle
Tickle
Tickle!
HA HA HA stop! I hate it

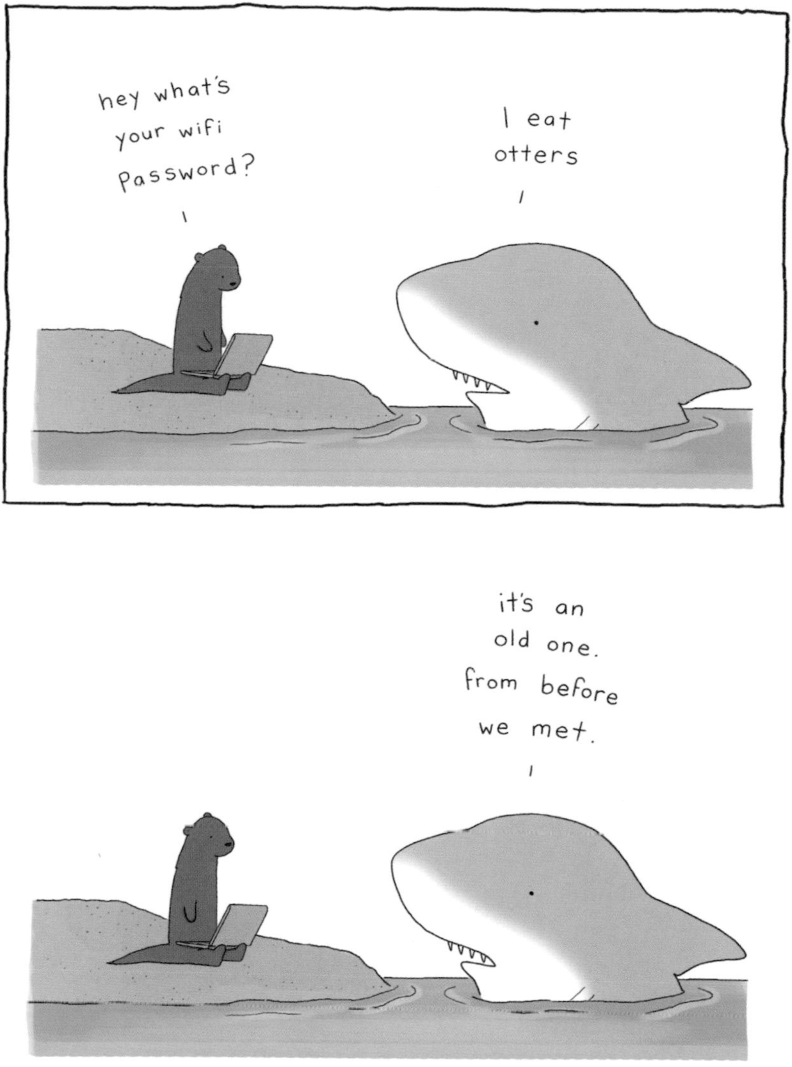
hey what's your wifi password?
I eat otters
it's an old one. from before we met.

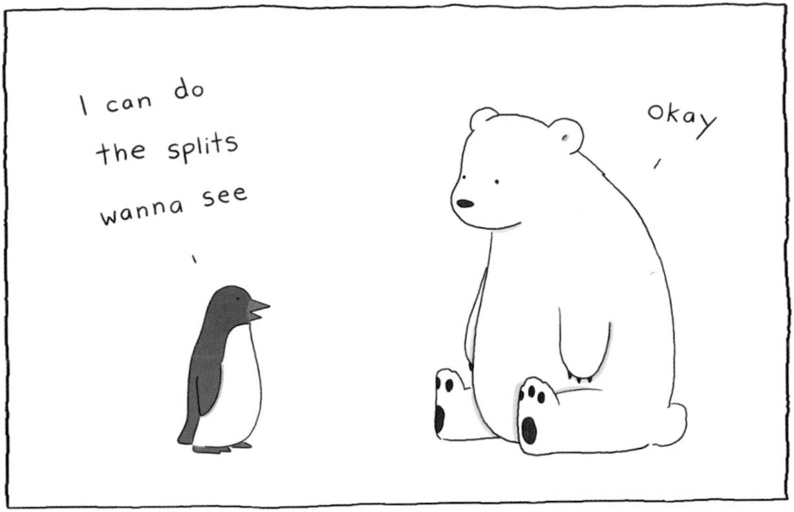
I can do the splits wanna see
okay

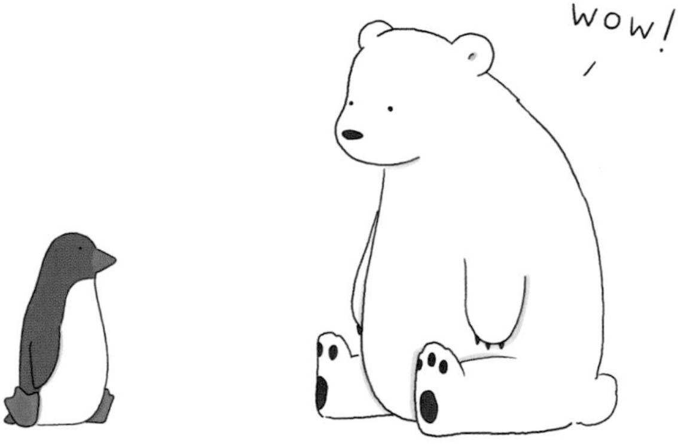
wow!

want me to make you a balloon animal?
okay.

OMG it looks just like me!

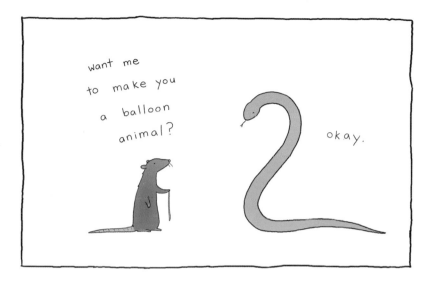

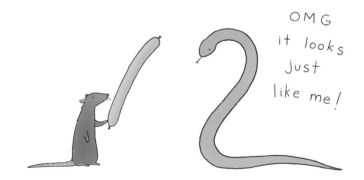

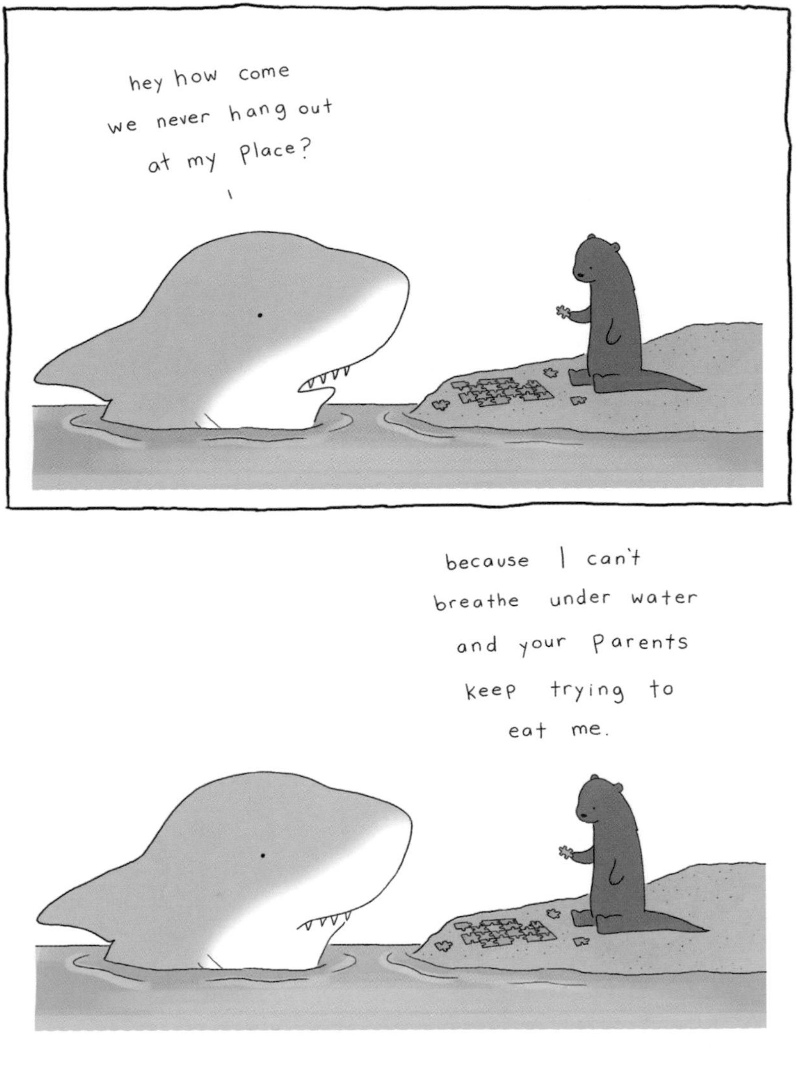
hey how come we never hang out at my Place?
because I can't breathe under water and your Parents keep trying to eat me.

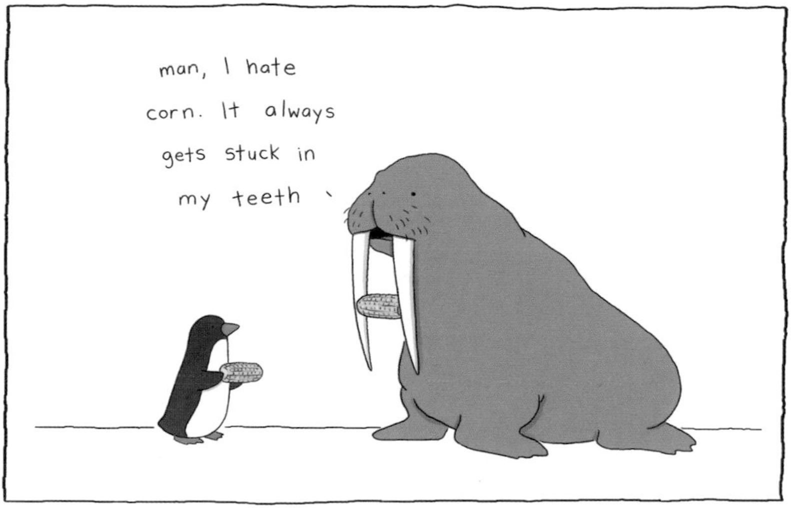
man, I hate corn. It always gets stuck in my teeth

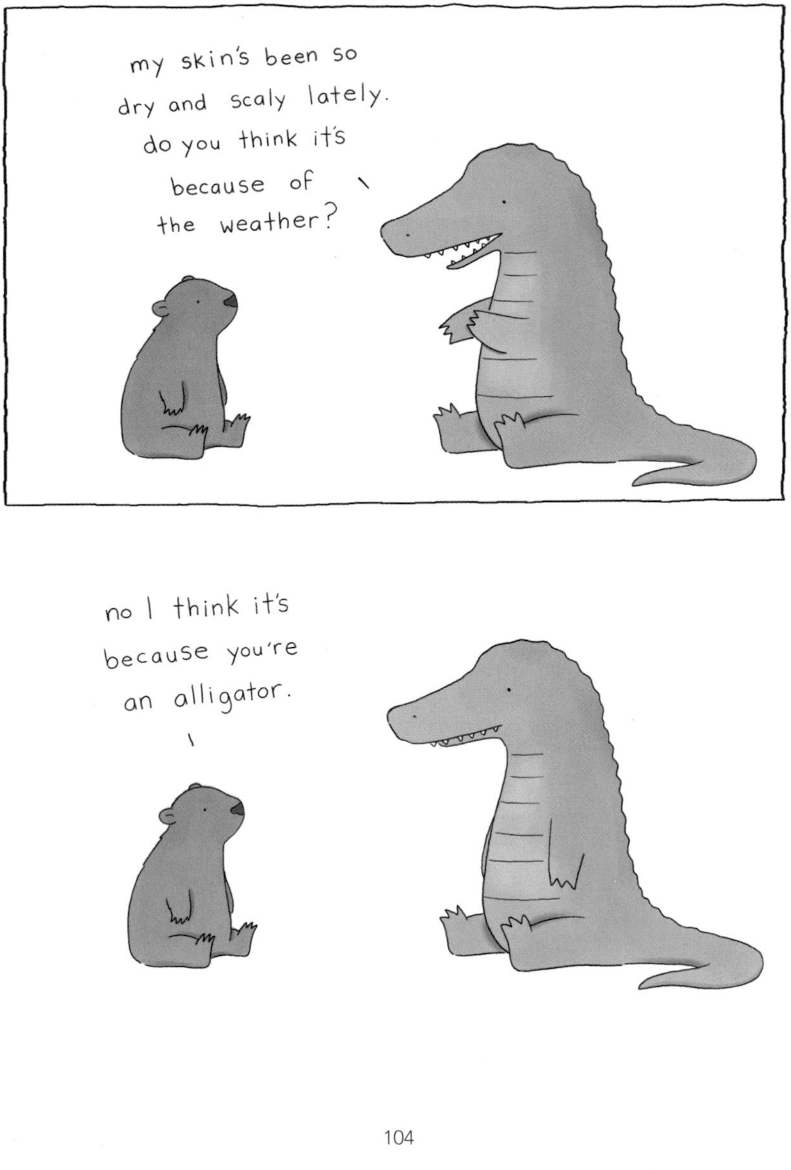
my skin's been so dry and scaly lately. do you think it's because of the weather?
no I think it's because you're an alligator.

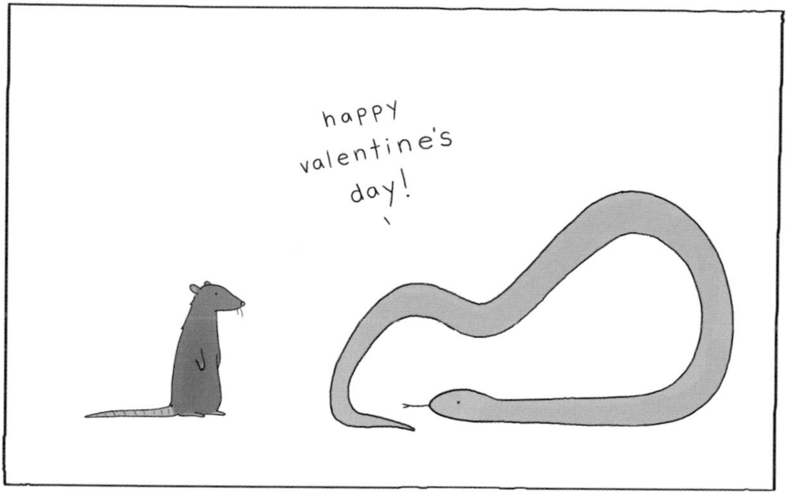
happy valentine's day!

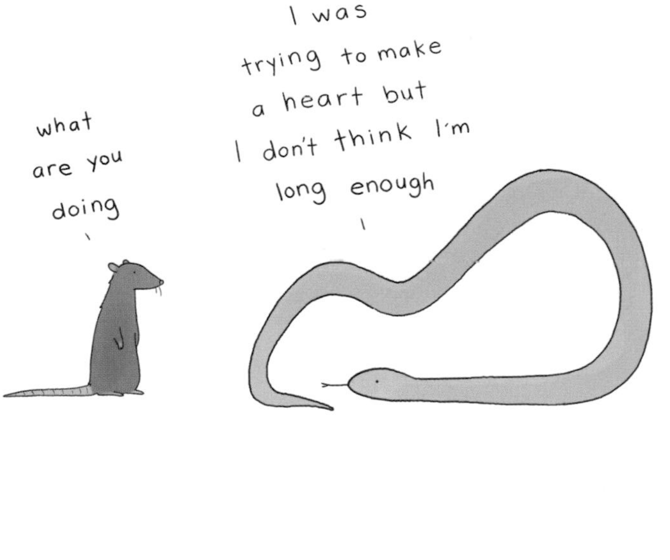
what are you doing
I was trying to make a heart but I don't think I'm long enough

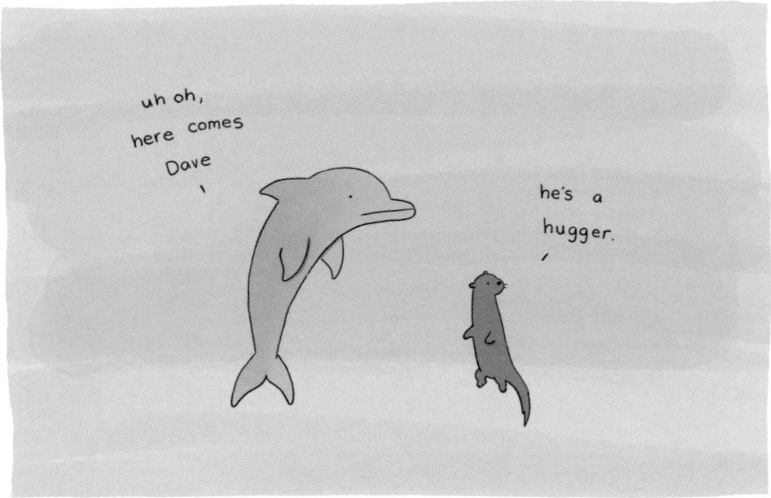
uh oh, here comes Dave
he's a hugger.

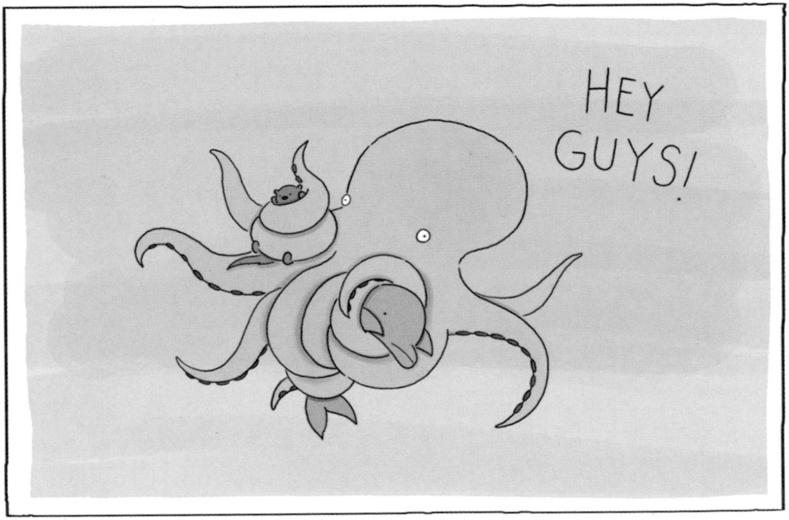
HEY GUYS!

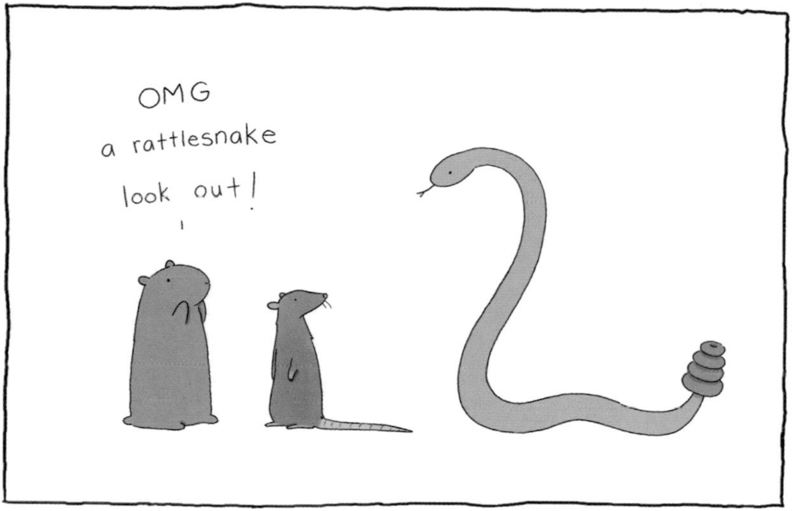
OMG
a rattlesnake
look out!

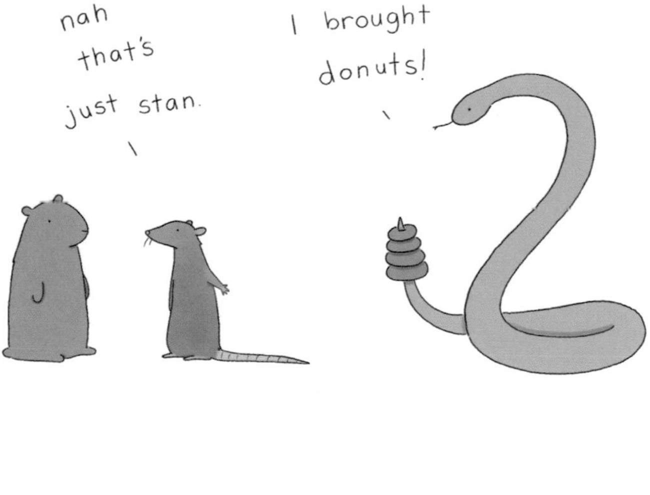
nah
that's
just stan.
I brought
donuts!

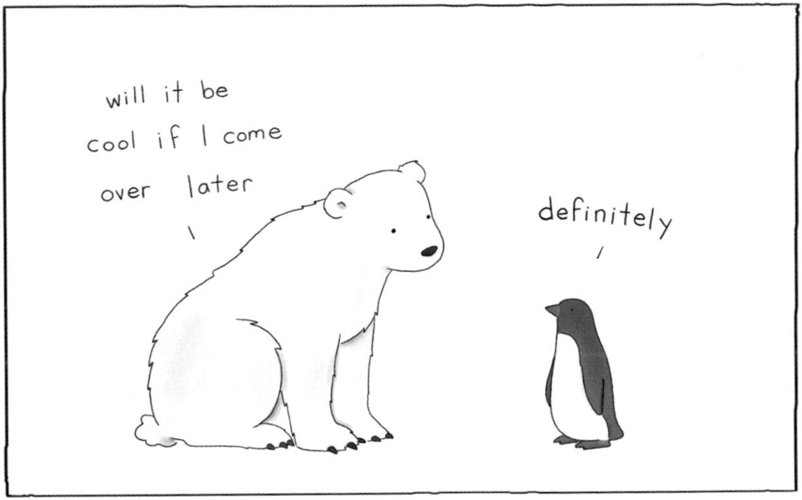
will it be cool if I come over later
definitely

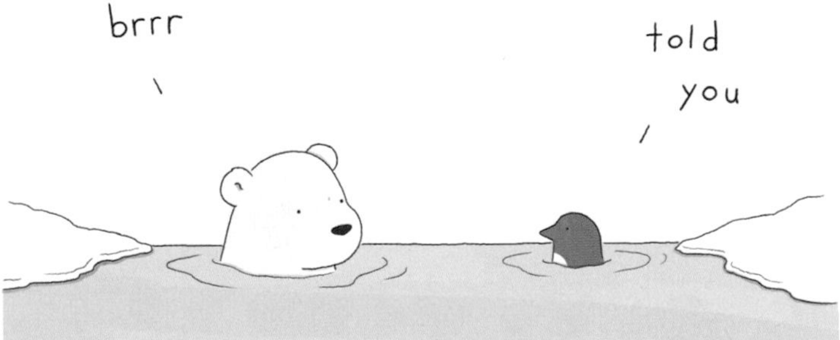
brrr
told you

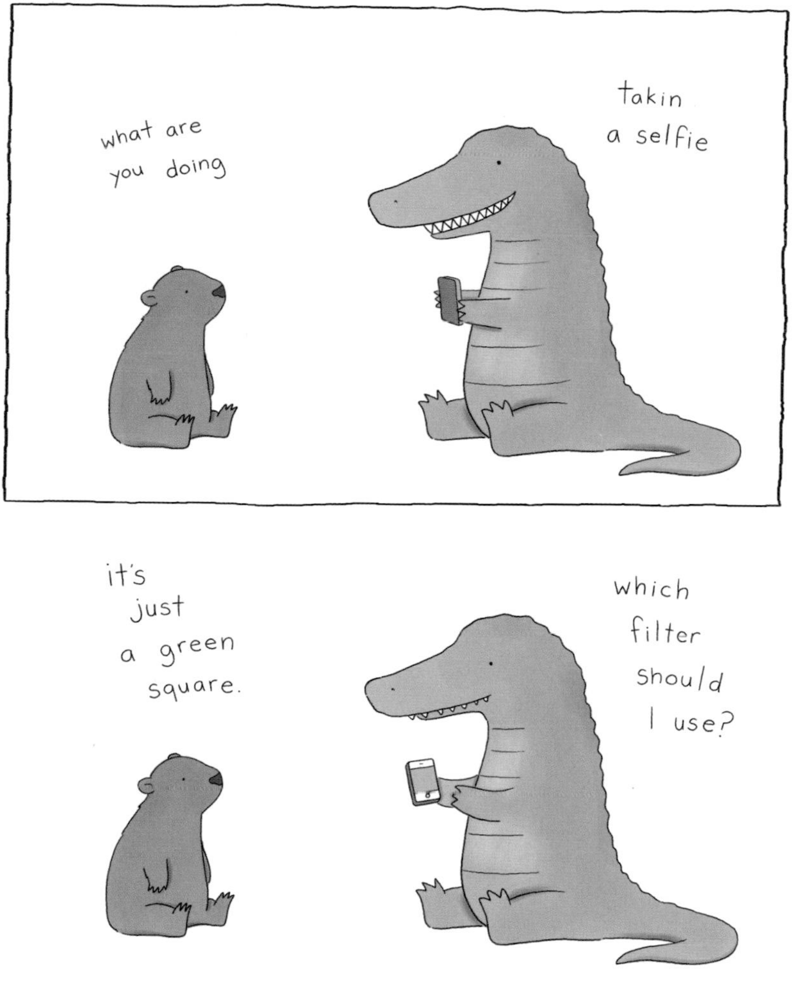
what are you doing
takin a selfie
it's just a green square.
which filter should I use?

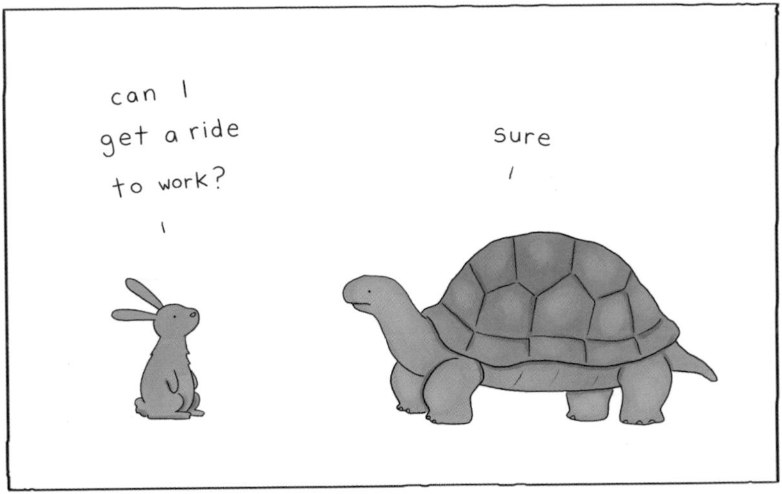
can I get a ride to work?
sure

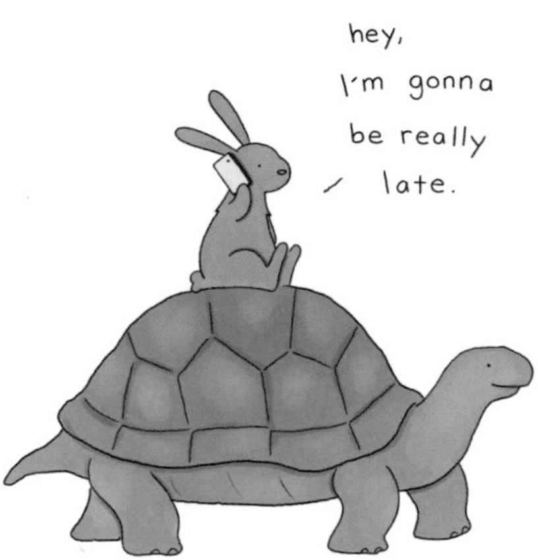
hey, I'm gonna be really late.

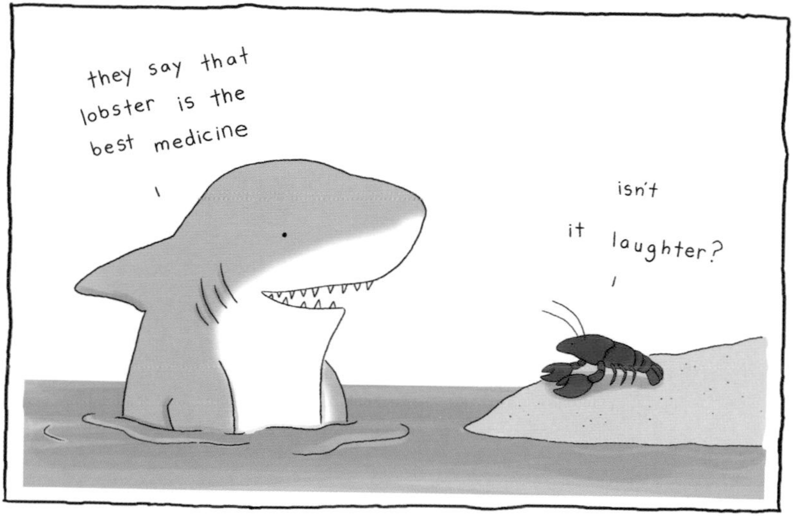
they say that lobster is the best medicine
isn't it laughter?

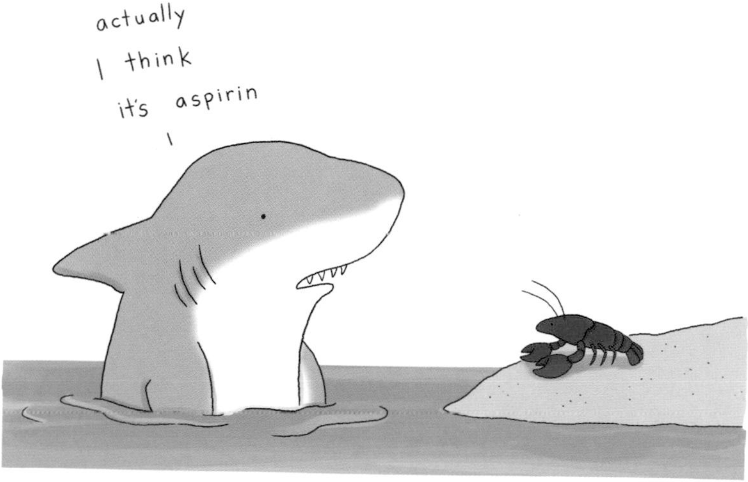
actually I think it's aspirin

Acknowledgments

I would like to thank my incredible agent Kathleen Ortiz for everything she has done for me, Joanna Volpe, Danielle Barthel, and everyone at New Leaf Literary, you have made so many dreams come true for me, and I am thankful for it every day. Jennifer Kasius, and the entire team at Running Press, for putting together another fabulous book. Roxy Lange, who continues to keep my baby (and me) company while I draw. My *Simpsons* family who have offered me so much support and inspiration over the past ten years, for which I am forever grateful. Those of you who continue to read these comics, thank you! I hope they make you happy. My dad, and my entire family especially the Climo, Heck, and Wilson families for their continuing love and support. For my brother and sister, two of my closest friends. For my mom, a great friend to so many, and to the friends she left behind who continue keep her memory alive. For my wonderful friend Mya, who I still talk to every day even though we haven't lived within 300 miles of each other in ten years. For my loyal friend Andrea, who stood by my side when nobody else would. For my loving friend Nikki, who is my touchstone in this vast city. For all of my friends, near and far, thank you for being in my life (and, while I'm at it, thanks to Facebook for making that possible). And finally, to Colin and Marlow, the loves of my life.